LANGUAGES AND LINGUISTICS

ECOWRITING: ADVICE TO ESL ON EFFECTIVE SCIENTIFIC WRITING IN ENVIRONMENTAL SCIENCE AND ENGINEERING

LANGUAGES AND LINGUISTICS

Second Languages: Teaching, Learning and Assessment
Ryan L. Jikal and Samantha A. Raner (Editors)
2009. ISBN: 978-1-60692-661-1

Critical Discourse Analysis: An Interdisciplinary Perspective
Thao Le, Quynh Le and Megan Short (Editors)
2009. ISBN: 978-1-60741-320-2

Critical Discourse Analysis: An Interdisciplinary Perspective
Thao Le, Quynh Le and Megan Short (Editors)
2009. ISBN: 978-1-60876-772-4 (E-book)

Building Language Skills and Cultural Competencies in the Military
Edgar D. Swain (Editor)
2009. ISBN: 978-1-60741-126-0

Building Language Skills and Cultural Competencies in the Military
Edgar D. Swain (Editor)
2009. ISBN: 978-1-60876-597-3 (E-book)

Aphasia: Symptoms, Diagnosis and Treatment
Grigore Ibanescu and Serafim Pescariu (Editors)
2009. ISBN: 978-1-60741-288-5

The Fundamental Structural Elements of Language: Operational Semantics
Giulio Benedetti
2010. ISBN: 978-1-61668-155-5

The Effects of Drugs on Verbal Fluency
Dario Zanetti, Maria R. Piras, Marinella D'Onofrio, Caterina F. Bagella, Paola Lai, Laura Fancellu, Susanna M. Nuvoli, and GianPietro Sechi
2010. ISBN: 978-1-61668-759-5

Speech Disorders: Causes, Treatment and Social Effects
Alan E. Harrison (Editor)
2010. ISBN: 978-1-60876-213-2

Building Strategic Language Ability Programs
Joshua R. Weston (Editor)
2010. ISBN: 978-1-60741-127-7

Bilinguals: Cognition, Education and Language Processing
Earl F. Caldwell (Editor)
2010. ISBN: 978-1-60741-710-1

Dictionary of Word Meanings
Hristo Georgiev
2010. ISBN: 978-1-60876-391-7

A Glossary of Second Language Acquisition
Iman Tohidian
2010. ISBN: 978-1-60741-941-9

Ecowriting: Advice to ESL on Effective Scientific Writing in Environmental Science and Engineering
Martin Mkandawire
2010. ISBN: 978-1-60876-425-9

Language Teaching: Techniques, Developments and Effectiveness
Carmine A. Hernandez (Editor)
2010. ISBN: 978-1-61668-834-9

Language Teaching: Techniques, Developments and Effectiveness
Carmine A. Hernandez (Editor)
2010. ISBN: 978-1-61728-077-1 (E-book)

LANGUAGES AND LINGUISTICS

ECOWRITING: ADVICE TO ESL ON EFFECTIVE SCIENTIFIC WRITING IN ENVIRONMENTAL SCIENCE AND ENGINEERING

MARTIN MKANDAWIRE

Nova Science Publishers, Inc.
New York

LIBRARY OF CONGRESS CATALOGING-IN-PUBLICATION DATA
Mkandawire, Martin.
  Ecowriting : advice to ESL on effective scientific writing in environmental science and engineering / author, Martin Mkandawire.
      p. cm.
  Includes bibliographical references and index.
  ISBN 978-1-60876-425-9 (hardcover : alk. paper)
  1. Environmental literature--Authorship. 2. Technical writing. 3. English language--Study and teaching--Foreign speakers. I. Title.
  GE35.M56 2009
  808'.066628--dc22
                        2009037471

Published by Nova Science Publishers, Inc. ✝ New York

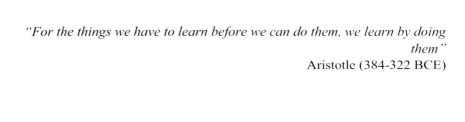

"For the things we have to learn before we can do them, we learn by doing them"
Aristotle (384-322 BCE)

For Chitsanzo and Chimango

CONTENTS

FOREWORD

Evaluation of scholarly achievement has eventually become the number of publications a scholar or an institution has. In order to publish, one needs to have adequate resources for research. To obtain research funding, one has to show recent publications, usually not more than five years old. Due to continued increasing of applications for research funding, on one hand, and shrinking recourses, on the other, competition for research funding has become very stiff. Consequently, funding institutions have narrowed the merit scale from mere number of scientific publication to impact factor (*IF*) of the journal in which the publications appeared. An impact factor is a simple descriptive quantitative measurement of a journal's performance derived from the average number of times articles from the journal published in the past two years have been cited in the current year. To publish in a high impact factor journal, there is need for a good research work, which requires good research resources. This is a viscous circle and dilemma for most academic and research institutions.

Our Tharandt Campus of *Technische Universität Dresden*, the Faculty of Forestry, Geo- and Hydro Sciences, has recently been criticised for low scientific publication output. This is despite that many institutes and scientists in the department have published in local German papers and journals; and every year, we pass many good research theses and scientific works. Most of these research works and theses can be high-level scientific publication. We, professors in the department, put all effort to encourage young scientists to write so that they can develop their careers. Yet the publication output is dwindling, continuously. The question, I have been asking is "why?" Slowly, I realised that many young scientists are eager to write and publish, but they do not. The reason is that they are neither lazy nor unwilling to develop their career, but reporting their scientific findings in another language – English – has grown rapidly into a barrier and it has became a challenge for most scientists, whom English is second language, to overcome.

It is undisputable that English has become a communication language for sciences. In the today's scientific world, we find that many scientists who use languages other than English are cutout from participating in the dynamism of scientific world. This has become a very big challenge to most scientists in countries where English is not a media of communication. Their voice and good scientific findings fail to reach the international scientific audience. Sometimes the same research findings published long time in non-English journals become hits when others publish similar in English journals. A good example is a story of Prof. E. Münch, a botany scholar of the 1920's in our campus (Tharandt) and later Munich University, who publish his work *Die Stoffbewergung in der Pflanze* (Translocation of nutrient material in plants) in 1930. The principles he described were much disputed in those days, but they have now turned to be very modern thought in plant science starting since the mid 1990 to present. The book was in German that it had very low circulation. This example shows that, many capable scientists do not get the recognition they deserve.

Certainly, publishing in local journals, which use languages other than English, has become less attractive because of low circulation, which results into low impact factor. This has forced us Germans and other non-native English-speaking scientists to write in English, and most journals that previously published works in German have turned to English too. Thus, reality is that we should learn to communicate our research work in English, a second language.

Tharandt, Prof. E. Gert Dudel

PREFACE

Despite going through a language course before joining the *Technische Universität Dresden*, it took me time to converse perfectly in German. I communicated with my colleagues mostly in English – more or less my native language – during the first years. On one hand, it was disadvantageous to me because I did not practice much of the German language, which I desperately needed. On the other hand, my colleagues took it as an opportunity to practise speaking English, and they had someone within reach to proofread their manuscripts before submitting for publication.

Proofreading and correcting English language for quality in scientific manuscripts was a challenge to me. Despite that I did a yearlong compulsory undergraduate course "English for Scientific Writing", I was still a novice in as far as communicating science in English was concerned. Nevertheless, my colleagues had very high hopes likewise expectations. Their expectations were an enormous challenge that had put me at a crossroads. On one side, I had contemplated to be frank with them and simply declare my incompetence in proofreading and correcting scientific work because I simply had no expertise. After all, my academic fields are neither scientific writing nor language editing. On the other side, my ego kept on telling me to meet the challenges and avoid losing the confidence. After all, a successful career in sciences requires good scientific communication skills. After a serious debate within myself, my ego overrode my passion for frankness.

Consequently, I decided to meet the challenges by indulging myself in a self-teaching process through reading guides on scientific communication and English for scientific writing. During this learning process, I compiled notes on principles of scientific writing. Eventually, I started identifying common problems of scientific writing in the manuscripts colleagues and students entrusted me with proofreading. Gradually, I developed interest to learn the main constraints which most scientists face when writing their works in a second language especially English. Then, I developed a habit of compiling flaws that frequently appeared in manuscripts and analysing their sources. I believed that pointing and suggesting means of overcoming the flaws would assist to improve scientific writing skills, which would give high changes especially to novice to publish with less hassle in English as second language.

Through the years and experience of correcting, proofreading and translating (between German and English), I have observed that many manuscripts from English as Second language scientists share a common set of problems. The problem originate from the similarity between native (e.g. German) and English languages in vocabulary but very different in grammar rules. As a result, many people fall in a trap of writing English in another language, into which I have sometimes fallen too, because of using German as my working language. On a number of occasions, my own manuscripts have been criticised heavily by reviewers due to poor language quality and style. This has resulted in rejections of some by some journals. Thus, I am not an exception from such mistakes.

Apparently, the need for effective scientific writing goes beyond us in the TU Dresden, or in Germany. Years of experience as a peer reviewer for a few journals (in geochemistry, environmental chemistry and engineering, ecotoxicology, aquatic sciences, just to mention a few) reveals that lack of effective scientific writing is common even among contributors from native English speaking, whom this book will hereinafter refer to as English as First Language (EFL). The lesson is that it is often difficult to identify problems in one's own writing, as it is difficult to remove a spec from one's own eye. Another thing I learnt was that there is more to good scientific writing than mere good knowledge of English grammar and good speaking skills.

This book is mainly based on these notes I collected from different sources during my self-teaching process; notes from common mistakes and flaws identified in manuscripts that I proofread and peer-reviewed; and, of course comments which peer reviewers made on my submissions. I chose the title *Ecowriting* for two reasons: to show that this book targets scientific writing for environmental sciences; and, to show figuratively the need for effective scientific writing that "ecologically or environmental sound."

Initially, I had no intentions to share my notes on scientific writing. However, through discussion with Prof. E. Gert Dudel, I came to realise that most of young scientists were so reluctant to write and publish their interesting research findings in international journals because of mere language barrier. Most young scientists are demoralised by frequent rejection of their manuscripts merely due to language quality. Yet, the number of publications has become a contemporary basis for success of scientific and academic career. Hence, I felt sharing the notes would help more people than just proofreading the manuscripts. Thus, this initiative is driven by an overriding passion to assist fellow novices to cope up with the "publish or perish" (POP) reality in the contemporary academia.

APPRECIATIONS

The interest to compile the notes into a book format came after Dmitry Tychinin of the Russian Academy of Sciences in Saratov invited me to co-author with him a few articles on English for scientific writing targeting contributors from the former Soviet block. I have enjoyed the field of scientific writing as an extra-curriculum because of the support and guidance from Prof. Dr. E. Gert Dudel and Prof. Dr. Wolfgang Pompe both of the *Technische Univedrsität Dresden*, who have also been hands that lifted me up when I really needed support to stand. Barbara Darr (formerly Taubert) provided some study material during my self-teaching. I also thank all who between 2000 and 2008 entrusted me with their works for proofreading as well as translating between German and English. Similarly, I thank several international peer review journals for involving me as a peer reviewer. I acknowledge the efforts of my wife, Msau, for collecting some of the examples used in this book. Prof. Dr. Pascal Kishindo and Prof. Dr. Edrinnie Kayambazinthu (of the University of Malawi), Steve Kamloni, and Msau Mkandawire read the first drafts and they made very constructive criticisms. Above all, I acknowledge invaluable support from our children – Chitsanzo and Chimango – who always correct my phonetics in German.

Dresden, Martin Mkandawire

BIOSCATCH

PD. Dr. Martin Mkandawire is a chemist specialised in environmental chemistry and engineering of aquatic systems. (PD stands for *Privat Dozent*, a German title equivalent to associate professor). Since 2005, he is a member of the Institute of Materials Science in the Faculty of Mechanical Engineering at *Technische Universität Dresden*. His researches include development of biocatalytic materials for bioremediation and biosensing in contaminated waters. Previously, he was a research associate in the Institute of General Ecology and Environmental Protection in the Faculty of Forestry, Geo- and Hydro Sciences in the same university for almost ten years. He researched in areas of biogeochemistry, ecotoxicology and bioremediation of radionuclides and metalloid in waters of uranium-mining sites.

Chapter 1

INTRODUCTION

For most scientists, success and recognition depends on the number of publications they have in prestigious journals. These publications help win support for the funding of new research projects, as well as aide in the development of their career. Unfortunately, peer reviewers may reject manuscripts of high technical and scientific content merely due to poor English, style, or format. A polished and fluent style of written manuscripts can significantly enhance the readability of a paper, which would ultimately assist in achieving rapid publication and an increase in future citations. Thus, the purpose of this book is to assist novice, as well as professional scientists, especially those who speak English as a second language, in optimizing their manuscripts. The actual goal is for users of this book to achieve a level of scientific writing that does not affect their acceptance for publication in a journal..

This chapter is intended to help readers use this book easily so that they can fully benefit from the information presented in it. It outlines the objectives of this book, and emphasises the need to strive to write with out errors. Additionally, a few terms in scientific writing, which appear in preceding chapters, are defined and briefly discussed. It is understood that this book may be very basic to some professional scientists, therefore, this chapter describes the intended target audience and scope of the book. Further, this chapter tackles specific issues in the field of scientific communication, which may be in the peripheral of most scientists who just want to use the book to publish their manuscripts quickly and easily in English language journals. Therefore, those interested in learning about specific areas for improving their scientific writing skills may skip parts of this introductory chapter and proceed to the specific chapter of interest.

1.1. WHY IS SCIENTIFIC WRITING ESSENTIAL?

Good communication is an essential skill for a successful scientific career because scientific research is not complete until the results have been published. Publishing scientific findings easily requires writing an accurate and easily understandable paper that conforms to some prescribed principle of presenting a scientific work to an audience; therefore, a good scientific communication skill is as important as the research itself to a career scientist. Good scientific communication skills require language proficiency and good writing skills, as well as good knowledge of the principles of scientific writing, which are prerequisites to producing manuscripts with few, or completely free of mistakes. Manuscripts with few mistakes are readily accepted for publication by reputable journals. Writing that is full of mistakes or difficult to read easily puts off readers; thus, most journals reject manuscripts that are written poorly, even if the reported research findings are major scientific breakthrough. This is due to the fact that the mistakes overshadow good scientific results. A manuscript is peer-reviewed before being accepted for publication in journals. Often, peer-reviewers are readers that do not possess enough background or knowledge of the research being reported; however, they are highly regarded by the editors of journals that their recommendations on manuscripts carry a lot of weight regarding the decision to publish the manuscripts. As readers, peer-reviewers can also be easily put off by mistakes that are avoidable in a manuscript, which can eventually force them to loose their objective evaluation of the scientific content [1]. As a matter of caution, peer reviewing is an extra workload that does not have any economic rewards. Further, some reviewers can be competitors in the scientific fields or areas.

Actually, submission of a poorly written manuscript can sometimes be construed either as laziness and carelessness, the authors' disrespect of their readers, or the incapability of improving writing [2-4]. Consequently, careless mistakes easily wash away the interest in reading the manuscript. Mistakes also give competitors an opportunity to recommend a manuscript not be published; therefore, manuscripts should be submitted with the least amount of mistakes as possible, if not without any mistakes. However, it is not simple to produce a manuscript devoid of mistakes, and not all mistakes are deliberate.

1.2. WHY SHOULD SCIENTISTS COMMUNICATE?

A critical aspect of the scientific process is the effective communication of ideas and research results to disseminate information to a larger community of scientists. This is referred to as scientific communication. The communication of scientific work contributes to the pool of knowledge within and across scientific disciplines, and very often provides information that helps others interpret their research results [1, 3, 5-8]. In fact, communicating science has many other practical reasons and benefits that include the following:

(i) To make a permanent, publicly accessible record of scientific research findings;

(ii) To avoid the unwarranted repetition in research efforts, by building foundation information for further or follow-up studies;

(iii) To convince research funding institutions to allocate even more resources for research;

(iv) To maintain the scientific ego and recognition because one's work is one's own epitaph; and

(v) The number of publications has progressively become an evaluation tool of career achievement in the sciences and in academia.

Above and beyond scientific communication, certain scientists also communicate with other groups in society aimed at building a sustainable relationship (e.g. journalists, schoolchildren, the public, the government, or the industry). This process of interaction between science and society belongs to the field of science communication, which is not the same as scientific communication.

1.3. AVENUES OF COMMUNICATION

Various avenues of communication are open for scientists to deliver information on their research and the results to their audience. The target audience and the purpose of communication are to determine the choices of the avenues. The audience can be categorized in to two avenues:

(a) Specialists, who read to partake of all its information; and,

(b) Casual readers, who are mainly interested in the results, or perhaps the experimental methodology employed as a background to their own work.

A few vehicles for addressing different scientific and general audiences and their purposes have been defined by Stepleton, et al. [9], which can be summarized as follows:

1   Research papers
    Purpose and features
    - To communicate new and original information to other scientists
    Target audience
    - Researchers and academicians within and outside the discipline
    - Research managers

2   Research review
    Purpose and features
    - An extended version of the discussion in a research article
    - To lead to the cutting edge of a given area of research
    Target audience
    - Researchers and academicians outside a discipline
    - Extension workers
    - Commercial interests

3   Conference paper
    Purpose and features
    - A brief presentation of objectives, methods, and the preliminary interpretation of research results
    Target audience
    - Researchers and academicians within and outside a field
    - Research managers

4   Thesis or dissertation
    Purpose and features
    - Written evidence of sustained research done over a considerable period, usually 2–4 years, for an academic award
    - Generally contains an extensive review of the literature, as well as the results of several experiments testing hypothesis
    Target audience
    - researchers and academician within a discipline

5   Book chapter
    Purpose and features

- To synthesize information about a particular subject
- Rarely sets out a fundamental hypothesis

Target audience

- Technical
- Same as research papers
- General
- Technicians
- Extension workers

6 Annual report

Purpose and features

- To describe activities and justify budget expenditures for a piece of research within a period of 12 months
- To spell out objectives, rather than to conclusively prove a hypothesis

Target audience

- Highlights
- Donors
- Policymakers
- Extension agents institutions directors
- Main text
- Researchers within and outside a field
- Research managers

7 Newsletter

Purpose and features

- To disseminate information of interest quickly in a readily digestible format
- The content carries little emphasis on justification or methodology
- Not a substitute for publication of research results in refereed journals

Target audience

- Researchers and academicians within and outside a field
- Extension agents
- Policymakers
- Expert ecologist and environmentalist including activists

8 Project proposal

Purpose and features

- To justify a programme of work and state the expected outputs
- To clearly define objectives of a programme

Target audience

- Research financiers and donors
- Policymakers
- Institution's directors

1.4. CHALLENGES OF SCIENTIFIC COMMUNICATION

1.4.1. The Classic Challenge

The classical challenge is the nature of science and scientific materials. Sciences are often hard to read because of the complexity of scientific concepts, data, and analyses. This is a challenge because writing in science may not be the same as writing a story, which on its own, may be entertaining. Thus, writing to communicate scientific work may look simple, but in order to produce a good scientific paper is difficult. A good research paper should attract and maintain the interest of the readers, should be understood easily, even by those outside the field, as well as non-scientists, while at the same time, communicating complex scientific findings. Hence, the challenge lies in achieving scientific papers that are attractive and interesting to read, even to readers in the peripheral of the scientific, field while communicating the research results and findings. Another classical challenge of scientific writing is achieving short and concise research papers. Keeping scientific writing pieces, short and concise helps reduce errors, and helps to keep readers interested in reading. A scientific paper should be like a woman's skirt – short enough, exposing the beauty, while covering the most important parts; when too short or too long, it is not attractive.

The fundamental purpose of scientific discourse is not the mere presentation of information and thought, but rather the actual communication. It does not matter how pleased an author might be to have converted all the right data into sentences and paragraphs; it matters only whether a large majority of the reading audience accurately perceives what the author had in mind. In summary, the classical challenge in scientific communication is for the authors to first put their readers in mind and understand how the readers go about reading.

1.4.2. The Contemporary Challenge

The contemporary challenge for modern scientists is to maintain ambition and courage to communicate their scientific findings to a wide audience. This is because the evaluation of success and achievements in a scientific career is based on the number manuscripts a scientist has had published in high impact factor or high citation index journals. Obviously, the scientists aim to reach the wider international community through primary scientific publications so that their articles have high citation and attain international recognition. The competition to address this wider scientific audience has become stiffer with the introduction of international recognitions and awards like the Nobel Prices, as well as the increasing competition for research funds. The English language is becoming a lingua franca for scientific communication because it is so widely used around the world, and it is a common second language among many diverse linguistic groups. As such, scientists must write in proper English to publish internationally. To prevail, a scientist should be recognized internationally., which simply means that scientists should write up their research findings in English to address an international scientific audience. This contemporary reality has forced scientists to look for ways to improve their English writing skills, thereby empowering themselves in the competitive environment of scientific publishing. Possessing perfect or near-perfect English for scientific writing increases the chances of having a work accepted for publication. This challenge becomes bigger when one is not a native English writer and contributor.

1.5. ENGLISH AS A SECOND LANGUAGE (ESL) CONTRIBUTORS

Scientists who do not speak English as their neither native nor first language are usually classified as "English as a Second Language (ESL)" writers in linguists, particularly English for the sciences. However, ESL writers or contributors may not necessarily have poor in English skills. Actually, observations made through a number of manuscripts, which the author of this book has peer reviewed, reveal that manuscripts submitted by most ESL contributors are easier to read and grammatically better than some of the manuscripts of those who are native English speaking scientist. This is because the former tend to mind grammar rules more than the latter. However, manuscripts contributed by most ESL scientists lack a logical flow of statements, as well as fragmented statements. This is attributed to their native language interfering with their English skills.

1.6. KINDS OF SCIENTIFIC WRITING

A scientist is likely to spend some time writing scientific papers, which often follow either the format of original research articles or literature reviews. Regardless of the genre, though, all scientific writing has the same goal of presenting data or ideas with a level of detail that allows a reader to evaluate the validity of the results and conclusions based on the facts presented. There are several different kinds of writing that fall under the umbrella of scientific writing. These include:

	Kind of writing	Scope
(a)	Peer-reviewed articles	Present primary research.
(b)	Grant proposals	Present research idea to prospective funding institutions.
(c)	Literature review articles	Summarise and synthesise research that has already been carried out.
(d)	Popular science articles	Communicate scientific discoveries to a non-scientific audience – science communication.

Any publication, a paper, a journal, or a thesis, is the author's last word on a particular topic. The editors determine the quality of a paper while the quality assurance is the responsibility of the journal reviewers. In an academic thesis, the supervisors determine the quality, while the thesis evaluation commission has the mandate to ensure quality.

1.7. TARGET OF THIS BOOK

This book intends to advise novice scientific writers in the field of environmental chemistry, engineering and technology, and of course, geosciences (i.e. eco-sciences). It may also be valuable for most professionals who wish to refine their scientific writing skills, despite their understanding of English and experience in scientific writing. Originally, the intended target groups were graduate students and scientists whose first language is German, within the Faculty of Forestry, Hydro-, and Geosciences (*Fakultät Forst-, Geo- und Hydrowissenschaften*) of *Technischen Universität Dresden*. However, the target has changed considerably through the years after the realization that most problems in scientific writing transcend beyond ESL to EFL contributors. Thus, the current aim of this book is to assist scientists in writing simple and natural texts while communicating complex scientific findings in a way that everybody, regardless of scientific background, can understand. The target of this book, therefore, includes even some native English writers who want to master an easy strategy to writing scientific papers and publishing in peer reviewed journal.

1.8. THE SCOPE OF THIS BOOK

Out of all available avenues, the scope of this book is mainly scientific communication for professionals intending to write scientific paper (either original research or review) for publication in international peer review journals. However, the advise can also be applicable to other available avenues, especially academic theses written in English by English as a Second Language (ESL) graduate students. This book addresses three major aspects of writing scientific papers. These include:

(i) A Fundamental knowledge prerequisite to a writing project in environmental sciences;
(ii) Writing sciences within universally accepted scientific writing styles, format, ethics, and language; and
(iii) The structure of scientific English, specifically to give English as a Second Language writers the tools needed to produce clear, complete, and comprehensive scientific articles.

In general, this book covers issues related to the structure of the language appropriate for scientific writing. Further, it provides advice on how to control individual components of the language structure for simple and clear scientific communication. The book also addresses specific aspects of writing that scientists, particularly those who speak English as a second language, face. However, on its own, this book is not complete because it does not deal with the basic issues of English grammar. In addition to merely understanding the principles of scientific writing, ELS writers should constantly read grammar rules because there is a tendency of writing in English as a native language. For instance, writing or speaking English in German grammar is very common, which has been termed "Deunglish" in certain quarters among academics. Further, both novice and professional scientific writers should learn from the writings of others. Scientific and technical writing is enhanced with reading literature and paying special attention to how other professional scientists write their work [5-7]. Generally, scientists improve their writing skills by repeatedly practicing reading, and writing, and commenting on what others write.

1.9. SPECIFIC SOURCES OF SCIENTIFIC WRITING ADVICES

The advice in this book is general. Various scientific medias utilize their own preferred formats and writing styles. Despite being narrow-scoped and very focused, most journals provide a summarized guide to authors. Mastery of the scientific writing style and format presented here will only enable novice scientific writers to adapt easily to most media specifics. Thus, this compilation is not sufficient, by itself, to make an accomplished writer. It does not teach one how to write in the English language, particularly in perfect grammar. Hence, novice writers must not only practice writing and thinking according to the advice given here. They should also consult other guides in scientific writing in general, as well as English grammar books. There are many guides on scientific writing currently available in book form, as well as electronically and through internet websites. Scientists, including professional writers, should now and then, and look at some of these guides. After all, this compilation is based on notes collected from many materials, including guides on general scientific writing available in other books, journal publications, and even websites (see appendix).

Chapter 2

WHAT TO CONSIDER BEFORE STARTING TO WRITE?

Before any scientist decides to communicate their scientific work to the scientific audience, there are a few things that they should be known and taken into consideration. Initially, the work should be well planned, and the target audience should be known in advance. In addition, there are few accepted scientific writing principles that should not be ignored. The basic principles of scientific writing should always be taken into consideration before embarking on writing, and strictly followed when finally writing the manuscript because otherwise, one may labour in vain. Thus, this chapter outlines a few rules of thumb and issues of effective scientific communication that should always be observed in writing a scientific work. Following this advice will definitely help novice, ESL writers, and even some professional writers, to reduce the chances of their manuscripts being rejected by journal editors. Above all, they will increase their effectiveness to communicate their research findings and scientific work an acceptable manner.

2.1. PLANNING TO WRITE

2.1.1. When to Start Planning

A good research paper needs to start with a good research question – a question to which the reader wants to know the answer [8]. Thus, planning to write should be concurrent with research planning and execution. Many scientists fail to publish papers from very successful research projects because the information and data gathered during the study is usually enormous, and the authors find it difficult to find a starting point. Sometimes precious time and effort is lost because less than 10% of the information or data generated in a research project is publishable. Some experts in scientific writing once wrote that many scientific writers have a hard time starting to write because they are intimidated by the huge project looming ahead of them [6, 8]. This often happens when the scientists want to report all results from a project in a single publication. To avoid this problem, large projects should be broken up into small pieces. The small pieces should be stand-alone studies that can be published independent of each other, and they (pieces of work) should cascade one another to answer the entire research question (i.e. they should be sequential steps to research). Similarly, the entire project hypothesis should be divided into sub-hypothesis capable of being tested separately. This is also the correct time to decide on the statistical analysis suitable for the data to test the hypothesis. In other words, the amount of data to be collected is already determined before executing the study. This way, planning of research writing should already indicate potential areas for publication. This reduces the collection of too much unnecessary information to be utilised in reporting.

2.1.2. Worthiness to Write

Once planning to write is thoroughly done and the research has generated adequate information (data), the scientists have the task to communicate the information or knowledge to a wide scientific community. When considering writing any paper, the first question that must be asked is: Is this study of sufficient interest to the profession that it warrants writing a paper? [3, 5]. Some research works that are done out of necessity (e.g. for academic degree thesis) can never be original, and this question should be asked at the outset, before much time and effort is spent writing an article that is not likely to be accepted for publication [10]. Usually, what warrants writing is the innovation research work brings and the new findings that were previously not known. Reporting work that is already known is a waist of time, and it is never interesting to read.

2.1.3. Deciding the Authorship of a Scientific Work

It is very important to decide the authorship of the scientific work immediately, after it has been found that the research work is worth publishing. In most cases, it is usually considered controversial whom to include as authors. Authorship of papers should be credited based on the following criteria [11, 12]:

§   **Criteria**
1   Substantial contributions to conception and design, or acquisition of data, or analysis and interpretation of data;
2   Drafting the article or revising it critically for important intellectual content; and
3   Final approval of the version to be published.

Therefore, the names that should be listed as authors must meet all three criteria. All other contributions, including analytics, data collection, and proof reading, should be mentioned in the acknowledgments [13, 14]. The convention of order of the authors' names [9, 15, 16] often dictates that:

§   **Rule of the thumb**
1.   The first author is the one who wrote the paper;
2.   The second and third were major contributors; and
3.   The last named may be the heavyweight, and possibly the guarantor – the person who takes responsibility.

Thus, the advantage of deciding the authorship before starting to write helps to assign and distribute tasks appropriately. As much as there is no specific rule regarding how many authors should appear on the paper, as a rule of the thumb, more than six authors is considered to be a lot.

2.1.4. Choosing the Audience to Address

Scientific and technical writing is written for a specific audience [5, 9]. Knowing the target audience helps the authors to decide what information to include. Authors would write a very different article for a narrow, highly technical, disciplinary journal, unlike when the target is a broad range of disciplines [17, 18]. In all cases, one must adopt the style and level of writing that is appropriate for the audience. Stylistic conventions and acceptable jargon vary tremendously from one field to another, and to some extent, from one journal to another [19].

2.1.5. Choosing an Appropriate Outlet Medium

After deciding the audience of the papers, the scientist should examine how the information can be communicated. In case they decide to submit to a journal, it becomes easier because they roughly know the target audience. Ideally, the chosen journal should have the maximum impact factor and citation index [20, 21]. Tables of impact factor and citation index can be obtained from most libraries, and on the Internet; however, it must also be considered whether the paper is appropriate to the style of that journal. Once a decision has been made, obtain a copy of the guidelines for authors from the respective journal and start writing the paper. This reduces work and time wastage because the drafts are written in the correct format from the beginning. This can save a great deal of time and effort because it avoids alterations at the end [8, 22].

2.1.6. Choosing an Appropriate Journal

Choosing a journal to submit a manuscript to requires careful thought. Some scientists leave this decision until the manuscript is ready; however, this is acceptable only when the scientists are experienced in publishing. In most cases, they do identify at least two potential journals to submit their manuscript to. However, it is easier to write the manuscript when already certain of the target journal, which is helpful to both new and even experienced scientists in publishing. Deciding early, before the writing begins, helps to meet the expectation of the audience readers. That way, one writes for the journal's audience.

There are numerous factors to consider when choosing a journal. It is unlikely that one journal will have all of the features, and a compromise is always necessary. However, there is one essential feature authors should not compromise on – manuscripts must be peer reviewed for publication if they are to be considered research articles.

The following rule of thumb will help scientists decide, the most appropriate and most suitable potential journal for the manuscript they are planning to write:

§	Rule of the thumb
1	The journal must be peer reviewed;
2	The journal must currently publish papers on the subject so that the authors themselves, when searching for papers like their own, they would first check in such a journals;
3	The journals must have the best reputation for publishing in the field. Thus, the journal editorial board should be composed of leaders in their fields, and the journal itself should be cited by others and probably with a high impact factor;
4	Preferably, but not a must, the journal should be published by a society because society journals usually have the largest circulation;
5	The journal should be indexed in at lease one of the major electronic databases such as Science Direct, Scopus, Medline, Biological Abstracts, Chemical Abstracts, or Current Contents;
6	The journal must have higher publication frequency, a low time lag between receiving and publishing papers.

Once a decision on a journal is made, the authors must obtain a copy of the most recent "author guidelines" of the journal. These guidelines must be followed explicitly, lest the publication of manuscript is delayed.

2.2. WHEN TO START WRITING

Do not wait until completion of all the analyses to start writing. The manuscripts should be separated into small discrete sections, a strategy sometimes known as "Parallel processing". In the Parallel processing strategy, one writes a section while completing the analyses for others. This helps writers to avoid burn-out [5, 8, 9, 23]. Writing and analysis for any given chapter, paper, or section is often an iterative process. Writing the results section of a paper is often the best way to discover the analyses and figures that still need to be done. At this moment, the overall organization of ideas is already outlined so that authors can work or concentrate on individual sections (see sections on how to start writing below).

2.2. BASICS TO KNOW BEFORE STARTING TO WRITE

2.2.1. Structural Format and Style

There is no single best way to prepare a scientific manuscript, except as determined by either the circumstances or audience for writing, or requested by the publisher [10]. Nevertheless, various scientific journals utilise different formats and writing styles to which each scientific writer should conform. Many formatting details can be learned by carefully modelling articles in journals. Thus, it is a good idea to acquire a few recent articles (because most journals revise the formats and styles constantly) from which the style and format can be learnt before starting to write. This is why choosing a journal in which to publish a manuscript should be done before starting to write. However, there are universal scientific styles and format issues to be considered.

There is no single ideal format of the manuscript found in scientific communication books. In most cases, it is a matter of choice and taste. However, most scientific communication books state that it is advisable to maintain only a single space after sentence terminators unless otherwise stated. The words must not be hyphenated at the end of a line. The title should be clear and concise. To maintain clarity and flow, the manuscripts should be divided into sections and subsections where possible, with clear headings and subheadings respectively. Titles and levels of headings (i.e. first heading, second heading, etc.) should be clearly indicated by either numbering or using different font styles. Usually, most journal editors reserve the placement of caption, figures and tables in the paper, but where the writers have the right to do so, the caption, figures and tables should be placed close to the text where they are referred. They should never be placed immediately after the section heading. All non-English words used in the manuscript should be italicised or be under inverted comas.

2.2.2. The Tense of Scientific Reporting

Problems of inappropriate or inconsistent tenses are common in writing. Many scientific articles contain mixed tense with the same paragraphs, ranging from past, past participle, to present and future tenses. Hence, the question is usually: What is the tense for scientific articles? Research papers reflect work that has been completed; therefore, use of the past tense throughout the paper, including the introduction section, when referring to the actual work that was done, including statements about your expectations or hypotheses. For this simple reasoning is why what the scientists, or others, did in the past should be stated in the past tense.

Example:
(a) I collected this data.
(b) Data was analysed using ANOVA.
(c) We hypothesised that toxicity of uranium in *Lemna gibba* is alleviated by the presence of phosphates

The past tense should be used, as well, when referring to the work of others that may be cited.

Example:
(a) Dudel, et al. (2000) found that water seeped through uranium, tailing heaps and contaminated ground water.
(b) Dudel, et al. (2000) wrote, "Water seeping through uranium tailings pose high contamination risk to water sources"

Events or objects that continue to happen or exist can be de scribed in the present tense

Examples:
(a) In this paper, I examine …
(b) The data rejects the hypothesis that ….

Events that will take place in the future can be in the future tense. What ever tense is chosen, it should be consistent through out the manuscript. Be careful in using "might", "may", and "would" (as in "this might indicate that ..."). In short, use past tense in the abstract, introduction, and method. The results and discussion sections can be in the present tense.

2.2.3. Use of Abbreviations

Many writers, in most cases to save space, use abbreviations. However, use of abbreviation in documents usually causes unnecessary confusion. Therefore, it is wise to use as few abbreviations as possible, if not avoid them wherever necessary. Generally, it is proper to use one, two, or three abbreviations in a document; however, use of more than four abbreviations in a document can be confusing. When abbreviating any terms, spell them out when used for the first time, regardless of the section, except for universally accepted abbreviations, such as Latin abbreviations and units combined with data. Never abbreviate units of measure when using them in a non-data context.

Examples:
(a) Abbreviating a term for first time:
    (i) Growth rate (μ) in *Lemna gibba* was monitored using Total Frond Area (TFA).
    (ii) Arsenate (As V) and arsenite (As III) are the most common inorganic arsenics in aquatic environment

b) Universally accepted Latin abbreviations:

	Abbr.	Meaning
(i)	cf.	Compare
(ii)	e.g.,	For example
(iii)	et al.	and others
(iv)	etc.	and so forth
(v)	i.e.,	that is
(vi)	vs.	versus, against

Note that except for "et al.", the Latin abbreviations should be used in parenthetic materials only. In non-parenthetic material, use the English translation.

(c) Unites with data and non-data:
    non-data   Length of root-like structures of *Lemna gibba* were measured length in millimetres
    with data   The roots were 50 mm long.

2.2.4. Intellectual Property

Prospective authors need to know the basics of copyright regulations or laws. This helps the authors to know how they can involve others people's ideas, work, and knowledge in their own writing. In short, nothing that is copyrighted can be used without the author's or publisher's consent. However, under conditions of "fair use", some copyrighted materials or portions may be used without prior permission from the authors or publishers. This is usually for non-profit educational purposes, because in an intellectual community, ideas are passed around freely. This is why, among academic's and scientist's fair use terms, authors can use pictures, graphics, quote or paraphrase text, but the source of the information is always to be acknowledged [24-26].

Most intellectual inquiry cannot take place without borrowing from the work of others. Naturally, even experienced writers rely on other writers, because their ideas are generated in the context of the ideas of others. As a matter of honour, they indicate their debts to other writers, and by doing so, they more clearly indicate their own original contributions [25, 27, 28]. In sciences, there is virtually no circumstance in which the findings of someone else cannot be expressed in ones own words with a proper citation of the source [24, 29, 30]. Thus, it important always to acknowledge the source of any materials copied elsewhere or downloaded from the Internet. Even when permission to use the material is granted, the author or source should be cited. This includes pictures, graphics, animations, movies, and even sounds. Failing to give credit or acknowledge the source is plagiarism. Plagiarism is turning in or passing off someone else's work as ones own [9, 23, 26]. The line between borrowing and stealing ideas or information is unclear. If authors know how to use and cite sources, and if they are careful to note borrowings when they are writing their paper, they will not have a problem with plagiarism. To be guilty of plagiarism is a very serious civil and criminal offence in most countries.

Plagiarism is frequently committed in the follow ways:

(i) Direct Plagiarism: Copying a source word for word for more than eight consecutive words without indicating that it is a quote and crediting the author [26, 28].

(ii) Vague or Incorrect Citation: Failure of authors to indicate where borrowing begins and ends, deliberate citation of a source incorrectly, and to indicate borrowings clearly [26, 30].

(iii) Mosaic Plagiarism: This is the most common type of plagiarism. The author does not copy the source directly, but changes a few words in each sentence or slightly reworks a paragraph, without giving credit to the original author [25-27, 30]. Thus, paraphrasing other's words too closely can also be construed as plagiarism in some circumstances.

These can also be regarded as types of plagiarism.

2.2.5. Fairplay in Intellectual Property

Any information that is taken from other works should be credited regardless of how it is used in the writing. Using borrowed information in writing can take several forms, such as quoting, paraphrasing, or summarising [24-27]. The most accepted form of accrediting the source of information in the intellectual sphere is citing the source and providing.

(i) Quotation

A word for word copy of something someone else has said or written. In writing, a quoted passage is indicated by putting quotation marks (") at the beginning and end of the quote. If the quote is long, the quote is set apart from the main text in an indented block. The quotation marks are omitted and the page number of the source is included in parentheses. The source of the quote must always be cited [24, 26, 31]. As a rule of thumb, approximately three to four quotes in a 10-page paper are about the upper limit.

(ii) Paraphrase

This is when authors restate in their own words something the source said or wrote. Many pieces of writing are almost all paraphrase [25, 30]. Paraphrasing, as opposed to quoting, puts the information in the design for the target audience. Putting something into your own words is an important intellectual activity in its own right; it shows that one understands and can work with the material. A paraphrase must always be cited, because putting something in one's own words does not make it is his or hers [26, 27, 31].

(iii) Summary

Like a paraphrase, a summary of a source is in your own words, but a summary is considerably shorter and does not follow the source as closely as a paraphrase. Again, authors must cite the source for the summary.

2.2.6. Gender Neutrality

Language and society reflect one another. Consequently, the changing roles of men and women in society have lead to the concern about the use of gender-biased language in technical and scientific writing [22, 32, 33]. Actually, gender-bias has become an important topic for modern writers of all disciplines [34]. Gender-fair language minimizes unnecessary concern about gender in the subject matter, allowing both the writer and the reader to focus on what people do rather than on which sex they happen to be [35]. Bias also tends to distract readers from the topic on which scientists are trying to inform them. There are three main types of gender-bias to be aware of, namely:

(i) Use of the term "man" to denote all people
(ii) Use of gender-specific pronouns to refer to people of either gender (i.e. he)
(iii) Subtle stereotyping of gender roles

Unfortunately, gender-bias can often go unnoticed by the writer. For instance, the practice of using "he" and "man" as generic terms poses a common problem. Rather than presenting a general picture of reality, "he" and "man" used generically can mislead the audience. On the other hand, replacing every "he" with "he or she" attracts even more attention to gender and defeats the purpose [8].

2.3. BASIC CHOICES TO MAKE BEFORE STARTING TO WRITE

2.3.1. Language Variety of Presentation

There are many varieties of English – American, British, Canadian, and Commonwealth English (spoken in former British empire in Africa, Australia and New Zealand) – which differ in accent, grammar, idioms, pronunciation, spellings, and style of writing [36-38]. While there are many more varieties of English, American and British English are the two common varieties that most journals generally accept. Of the English varieties one is neither correct nor wrong but, there are certainly preferences in use. However, mixed usage of different English varieties results in difficulties to follow the writing. Hence, the most important rule of thumb is to choose a variety of English to maintain throughout the manuscript. For instance, once the authors decide to use American English, then they should consistently observe spelling, terms, and construction regulations of the American English. This is of course, not always easy, but it is possible.

2.3.2. Person of Presentation

If there is one stylistic area where scientific disciplines and journals vary widely, it is the use of first or third person constructions in the manuscripts. For a long time, it had been recommended that the third person should be used in scientific writing because it brings neutrality to the manuscript. However, some journals (e.g., environmental engineering and ecology) have moved away from a very strict adherence to the third person construction, and permit limited use of the first person in published papers [1, 8, 10]. Nature Sciences Journals and Newsletter, as well as Science Publication, commonly use the first person. The rule that scientific writers must avoid personal pronouns is old, and it is being rejected by many modern scientific journals [5, 10, 39]. Nevertheless, many disciplines still prefer the third person construction. As it stands currently, it is up to the authors to choose the persons of reporting. Once it is decided, the person should be maintained, even though restricted mixing may be allowed depending on the situation. Generally, it is advisable to avoid excessive use of the terms *I*, *me*, and *my*, as well as the phrase "*personally speaking*". Specifically, it sounds unprofessional to use first person in the *Introduction* and *Discussion* sections. Use of the first person should be sparingly, if at all, and its use should be avoided in the results.

2.3.3. Voice of Reporting

Many scientific writing guides encourage writers to write in an active voice, shunning the passive because the active voice is shorter, more direct, and more dynamic than the passive voice [40]. However, sometimes the active voice is awkward or inappropriate. The use of the passive voice in scientific research reports keeps the spotlight focused on the experiment itself, rather than the researchers. When writing, try to find all passive sentences and change them into the active voice, except those sentences for which the passive voice is an improvement [8, 17, 22, 33]. The passive voice can be recognized by a "double verb", and is formed by using a form of the verb "to be", and the past participle of another verb [40].

Example:
Active   *Lemna gibba* accumulates uranium and arsenic at a higher rate than *Eleocharis dulcis*.

Passive Uranium and arsenic were accumulated by *Lemna gibba* at a higher rate.

However, there are exceptions, where passive is regarded appropriate.

Example:
Active We conducted the experiments with *Lemna gibba* in semi-continuous culture mode.
Passive Experiments with *Lemna gibba* were conducted in semicontinuous culture mode.

2.4. HOW TO START WRITING

The first task to accomplish as one begins the process of writing is to order and organize the information to present. Some writers work well from an outline, others do not. Some write first to discover the points, and then rearrange them using an after-the-fact outline. What ever process one may use, be aware that scientific writing requires special attention to order and organization [8, 22, 33]. Scientific papers are usually divided into sections, thus, one needs to know what information will go into each. On this occasion, one should at least develop a list of the major points to be included in each section before he or she begins to write. If the paper has multiple authors, then this is a good time to work with collaborators to ensure that all the points the group wants to make are listed.

2.4.1. Organization of Ideas

Before embarking on actual writing, first make an outline of the major headings (see development of an effective outline below). List the key ideas to be covered under each heading [1, 3, 5, 32]. Organize the thoughts and the logic of the arguments at this level, not when trying to write complete, grammatical, and elegant sentences.
There are three steps to be followed, which are summarized as follows:

§   **Step**
1   Figuring out what to communicate
2   Planning the order and logic of the arguments

3   Creating the exact language in which to express the ideas

Many authors find it useful to attach page lengths and time lines to each subsection when making an outline [8, 22]. Such time estimates are usually inaccurate, but the process of establishing them is quite useful [1, 3, 5, 32]. Commence the writing by expanding the outline section-by-section. Usually, ideas for later sections come while writing earlier ones. This is especially useful for filling out the structure of a "Discussion" while writing the "Results" (see writing a scientific paper section). By the time one writes the "Discussion", the outline has usually been fleshed out substantially, and most of the topic sentences are present in note form [1, 3, 5, 32].

2.4.2. Deciding on the Data to Present

It is important to organize the data to present in the manuscript before the actual writing of the first draft of the manuscript starts [41]. At that juncture, authors should decide the results to present and how best the results can be presented, by paying attention to whether data is best presented within the text or as tables or figures.

In case the authors decide to present their results in form of either a table or a figure, the preparation of the tables and figures, their titles and legends, and appropriate statistical analysis should be done and laid out before beginning to write the first draft of the manuscript. This approach has two very important advantages:

1. The authors are certain of their results before they need to interpret them; and

2. The authors are also able to determine the actual and specific data that answer the questions posed in the research. This helps avoid presenting unnecessary data and information, and above all, wasting of time.

2.4.3. Developing an Outline

Once the ideas have been organized and the data or results to present have been decided upon, authors should develop an outline of their prospective manuscript. Preparing an outline is a very important step in the process of producing a manuscript. The outline bears roughly the same relation to the final manuscript as an architectural blueprint does to a finished house [22, 42]. Its purpose is to divide the writing of the entire paper into a number of smaller tasks. A good outline organizes the various topics and arguments in logical form [1, 17, 42, 43]. Logical formatting assists the authors to identify, before writing the manuscript, any gaps that might exist.

Authors need to put down some notes to guide their thinking. As a rule of thumb, the following steps should be considered before beginning to write the manuscript:

#	Step
1	Prepare a central message sentence with 20-25 words. Everything in the manuscript should be written to support the central message. The central message sentence should encapsulate the most important findings.
2	Briefly, state where the scientists worked (i.e. laboratory, field trials, or field survey), the materials they used, and most importantly, the methods they used to carry out the study.
3	Summarize the question(s) and problem(s): What was known before the study started? What answers were needed to address the problem(s)? What are the key points pertaining to the question(s) and problem(s), likewise, what are the things done to answer the question(s)?
4	Define the principal findings and results. Expand the most important findings encapsulated in the central message sentence. Additional finds should also be included at this point. List them in note form, regardless of the order or the number put down.
5	Describe the conclusions and implications. Make brief notes on each of the implications that arise from the study. What are the principal conclusions of the findings? What is new in the work and why does it matter? What are the limitations and the implications of the results? Are there any changes in practice, approaches or techniques that would be recommended?
6	Organize and group related ideas together, and then, list each key point separately, arranged either chronologically, or by order of importance. Identify the important details, describe the principal findings, and provide the analysis and conclusions that contribute to each key point.
7	Identify the references that pertain to each key point

2.5. Prerequisite Knowledge for Writing

There are a few prerequisite principles of writing that every author is requested to know before embarking on a writing project. Knowledge of the principles helps writers to write effectively and with precision. When the principles are followed strictly, chances of negative evaluation of the manuscripts reduce considerably. Hence, this section introduces some of the most important principles of scientific writing.

2.5.1. Presentation of Figures and Tables

Style of presentation of figures and tables is publisher or editor specific – each publishing institution or editor has its own preferred style. In this book, details of presenting figures or tables have been tackled in detail in the next charter. Nonetheless, authors are obliged to know the standard scientific regulation regarding the presentation of figures and tables before embarking on the actual writing of the manuscript. For instance, each figure and table should have a caption. Captions should not merely name a table or figure, but they should contain sufficient information so that a reader can understand a table or figure, in most cases, without referring to the text [1, 5, 8, 9, 23]. Captions are often most effective when they briefly summarize the main result presented in the table or figure. For figures, it is preferred that the caption be under the actual figure, while in tables, the action is recommended to be on top of the actual table.

2.5.2. Presentation of Numbers and Data Quality Assurance

When writing numbers in text, the numbers zero through nine should be spelled out, except when it is a table or figure number, or a metric measurement [7, 23]. The numbers 10 and above should be written in Arabic numerals. Capitalize nouns followed by numerals or letters that denote a specific place in a numbered series [6-9].

Examples:
(a) Add four drops of 20 mg L^{-1} $NaHCO_3$ to the solution.
(b) Select 30 fronds at random, and inoculate into the medium.

(c) As indicated in Figure 3, toxicity of uranium to *Lemna gibba* correlates negatively to phosphorus content.

Note that there are some exceptions; for instance, spell out any number when it is the first thing in a sentence, and in the abstract, use digits for all numbers, except when they begin a sentence.

Example:

Inappropriate	30 fronds of Lemna gibba were inoculated randomly
Appropriate	Thirty fronds of Lemna gibba were inoculated randomly.
Appropriate in abstract only	We added 4 drops of 20 mg/L NaHCO3 to the solution

All measurement reporting should be done in the recommended international standard (*SI*) units. Try to be consistent with number formats. That is, if a series of related numbers are being reporting, they should all be presented with the same number of decimal places.

2.5.3. Structure of Paragraphs

A major difficulty seems to be how to organize sentences into effective paragraphs. A paragraph should begin with a topic sentence that sets the stage clearly for what will follow [7, 10]. Make topic sentences short and direct. Build the paragraph from the ideas introduced in your topic sentence and make the flow of individual sentences follow a logical sequence. The first sentence of a paragraph must be independent, i.e. able to stand on its own.

Example:

    Consider   Much as these studies are important, there is...

This sentence would be correct in the middle of a paragraph, but as the first sentence, it should more appropriately read:

While studies of the effects of uranium and arsenic on *Lemna gibba* growth rate are important, there is ...

Many authors try to finish each paragraph with a sentence that forms a bridge to the next paragraph [10]. Paying attention to continuity between paragraphs is a good idea; however, such sentences are often better as a topic sentence for the following paragraph than a concluding sentence of the current one.

It is nice to conclude a paragraph by recapitulating its main points and anticipating what follows, but authors should avoid statements of conclusion or introduction, which contain no new information or ideas [1, 5, 8, 9]. Paragraphs that contain only one or two sentences are rarely good because they cannot develop ideas adequately. Two-sentence paragraphs usually represent either misplaced pieces of other paragraphs, or fragments of ideas that should be removed or expanded.

2.5.4. Clarity and Conciseness

As has been mentioned several times, the aim of writing and publishing is to communicate scientific findings clearly to others [44]. The probability of the development of unscientific work is considerably reduced when written briefly and straight to the point. Therefore, brevity should be exercised by stating what is meant clearly in the simplest form, and by avoiding decoration with unnecessary words or phrases. Clear and concise writing can be achieved by avoiding use of long words where short ones would do. It helps to write simple and short sentences that can be connected later [44-46]. Simple sentences are easier to connect to make long sentences later than it is to break long sentences into simple sentences. Each sentence should completely consist of a clear subject and predicate [44-46].

2.5.5. Preciseness

Scientific terminology carries specific meaning, thus authors should use scientific terminology appropriately and consistently. A critical function of technical terminology is to say a lot with a few words, for instance, *ecotoxicology* means the study of the movement of toxic materials through the environment, and the effect that those materials have upon natural systems, in particular, the effects on populations and ecosystems. The "movement" referred to relates not just to the physical movement of toxic materials, under the influence of groundwater flow, for example, but also the movement through plant and animal populations via the food web. This applies, as well, to appropriate acronyms (e.g., ICP-MS, AAS, PCR, etc) and abbreviations. Direct the paper toward the average reader in the intended audience. If the target audience of the writing were a highly technical journal, it would necessarily use the technical jargon. If the target is a general science audience, jargon should be strictly limited. Where the use of scientific or technical jargon cannot be avoided, authors should take time to explain them in the simplest way possible.

2.5.6. Coherence

Some very interesting research works may fail to be appreciated despite presenting the most interesting results because the writing does not "flow and resonate." Articles that "flow and resonate" influence the readers more than the equivalent message presented in a form that is merely clear [4, 7, 17, 43]. To achieve flow and resonation in writing, it is advisable that topic sentences are first organized in point form in a logical sequence in which one builds on what came previously. Then restructure the text so that it follows a sequence. Write topic sentences that state the key issues for each point concisely and without jargon. Flesh out each paragraph with a carefully constructed sequence of sentences that builds the intended argument. Make sure there is adequate conceptual 'glue' between paragraphs and major sections. Lead the reader along so there are no surprising jumps in the subject. The reader should anticipate the next subject before they get there.

2.5.7. The Two Don'ts of Scientific Writing

In order to make a scientific paper interesting to read, authors should allow their readers to participate actively. Readers are active participants in reading a paper when they are given freedom to make their own evaluation on issues or results being discussed in the paper. When enough freedom is given to the readers, the readers feel respected and enjoy reading the paper. Actually, readers do not simply read, but they interpret and make many of their most important interpretive decisions about the substance of the work based on clues from work's structure [47]. Hence, most readers do not like to be forced to believe in something or be indoctrinated.

The freedom to participate is allowed when the two "don'ts", outlined below, are part of writing:

i. Do not tell but show the audience

Authors should show the readers how the results are interesting or significant, rather than telling the reader that a result is interesting or significant [42]. Similarly, do not describe a result, but show the reader what they need to know so that they can come to their own conclusion about it [6, 7]. Wherever possible, avoid words that evaluate, like "this result is important ...", or "the findings are interesting ...". It should be up to the reader to evaluate whether the result is important or interesting. Example:

| Inappropriate | The large difference in uranium immobilisation between culture with and without Lemna gibba is particularly interesting |
| Appropriate | After 21 days, the culture inoculated with Lemna gibba reduced uranium from 1000 to 250 µg L-1, while there was no reduction in the non-inoculated culture. |

ii. Do not report the data or the statistics, but the results

Authors should refrain from focusing on discussing the content of the tables and figures, but they should focus on discussing the results that the table and figure help to clarify [5-7, 9]. The tables and figures should be used only to illustrate points or clarify results in the text; thus, tables or figures should never be the subject of the text. Further, scientific results should always be differentiated from the methodological tools used to support and present the results. Example:

| Inappropriate | Figure 4 shows the relationship between the accumulation of arsenic in *Lemna gibba* and phosphate concentration in the culture media |
| Appropriate | The high of accumulation of arsenic in *Lemna gibba* was inversely related to phosphorus concentration in the culture medium (Figure 4). |

2.5.8. Putting Readers' Expectations First

The fundamental purpose of scientific discourse is not the mere presentation of information and thought, but rather its actual communication. It does not matter how pleased an author might be to have converted all the right data into sentences and paragraphs, but it matters only whether a large majority of the reading audience accurately perceives what the author had in mind [47]. Therefore, authors should understand how readers go about reading because readers have specific expectations from a written scientific work. Authors should always put interplay between scientific substance and presentation structure in order to meet the readers' expectations. Every reader enjoys a work that is presented in the simplest form, which facilitates easier interpretation of the information presented. For instance, a study has shown that data presentation affects and influences the reader's expectations very much [47].

Examples:

In the study, a team of communication scientists gave formats of data presentation to their survey respondents as follows:

a) Format One: a number of written structures [47]

t(time) =15', T(temperature)=32°, t=0', T=25°; t=6', T=29°; t=3', T=27°; t=12', T=32°; t=9'; T=31°

b) Format Two: tables [47]

(a)		Or	(b)	
Time (min)	**Temperature (°C)**		**Temperature (°C)**	**Time (min)**
0	25		25	0
3	27		27	3
6	29		29	6
9	31		31	9
12	32		32	12
15	32		32	15

c) Format Three: graphic

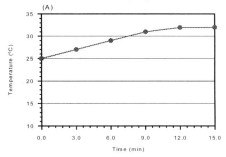
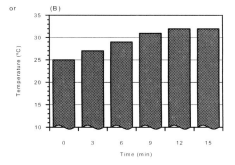

The same information appears in three formats, yet most readers found the third the easiest to interpret, and the second format the second easiest to interpret. Thus, an author who presents data in either graphic or tabular format concurs with the readers' thoughts in this example. The graphic and tabular structures indisputably are easier to read, interpret, and understand.

Information is interpreted more easily and more uniformly if it is placed where most readers expect to find it. These needs and expectations of readers affect the interpretation, not only of tables and illustrations, but also of prose itself. Readers have relatively fixed expectations about where, in the structure of prose, they will encounter particular items of its substance. Therefore, authors should be consciously aware of these locations so that they can better control the degrees of recognition and emphasis a reader will give to the various pieces of information being presented. For this reason, the prose has shape. A research article, for example, is generally divided into recognizable sections, and usually labeled Introduction, Experimental Methods, Results, and Discussion. When the sections are confused – when too much experimental detail is found in the Results section, or when discussion and results intermingle – readers are often equally confused. If these structural expectations are continually violated, readers are forced to divert energy from understanding the content of a passage to unravelling its structure. When the possibility of misinterpretation or no interpretation increases dramatically, the complexity of the context is high.

2.6. CHAPTER COMPENDIUM

The idea to write and communicate the scientific work is part of the planning of research. Thus, it is important that the research should be interesting and exciting. This may seem like an obvious step, but there are a couple of problems with the way scientific research is often reported. Interesting does not necessarily mean new, but rather its relevance to the readers. Once, the interesting research is conducted, it is up to the authors (communicators) to show why and how it is interesting. There are many reasons a research study can be interesting, however, there is no formula for deciding what is interesting about an article. Often the authors' first instinct about an article is right. Thus, authors should decide on how to make the research and article interesting to prospective audience. Whatever the authors decide on, that is where they should begin to write; however, they should avoid being obsessed with only making the research seem interesting. The goal of writing or reporting the research should not only be to pass peer review, but it should also hook readers and show them why the research was exciting.

A paper is interesting when the authors let the research speak for itself. Most readers are interested in details about the research process. They do not just want to know the researchers' conclusions, but they want to understand for themselves how the research was done. When writing about a scientific study, avoid the temptation to gloss over details about methods, to omit the data the study produced, or to ignore other relevant studies the authors mention in their introduction. Thus, if part of the research is to be reported or published, details of the procedure during the research should be documented.

Even though journal articles follow a predictable pattern, with an Introduction, Methods, Results, and Discussion, this does not mean authors cannot start with other sections, like Methods, in the write-up.

Chapter 3

HOW TO REPORT A SCIENTIFIC WORK?

Scientific work is communicated to the larger communities through different communication avenues (e.g. project reports, book chapters, conference presentations, or journal contributions) (see appendix 1). Writing for all but project reports are categorized as either an original research report, which communicates specific new scientific findings, or a research review, where previous research works are integrated and evaluated in order to clarify a particular problem or issue [5, 6, 8, 9].

3.2. WRITING PROJECT REPORTS

Project reports are usually written to the specifics of the project-funding organization. Thus, there is no special format and style for these types of scientific communication, and such reports require their own types of guides – they are beyond this compilation of advice. Therefore, this compilation is limited to discussing writing an executive summary of this type of scientific communication. Nonetheless, the whole discussion in this compilation may also benefit the general writing of project reports.

3.2.1. Writing the Executive Summary

Executive summaries are much like other summaries in that their main goal is to provide a condensed version of a longer report's content. The key difference, however, is that executive summaries are written for people who most likely do not have time to read the original. An executive summary should be referred to as an abstract because there are major distinctions between the two. An abstract is a shortened form of a work that retains the general sense and unity of the original [2, 32, 48]. An executive summary goes beyond this; it seeks to let the reader in on what the real significance of the report is to which the reader is expected to respond to [2, 9, 32]. In short, the purpose of an executive summary is:

(a) To preview the main points of your document, enabling readers to build a mental framework for organizing and understanding the detailed information in your document; and

(b) Helps readers determine the key results and recommendations reported in the document.

Some rules of the thumb when writing the executive summary [48] are:

§	Rule description
1	The executive summary should be no longer than 10% of the original document. It can be anywhere from 1-10 pages long, depending on the report's length.
2	Executive summaries should be a self-contained and stand-alone document. Although this may not always be the case - for this assignment, executive summaries should make recommendations.
3	They should be accurate because people who have not read the original will make decisions based on the summary.
4	Executive summaries should not be written until after the research is finished. Before writing the summary, the following are necessary: (i) To scan the research to determine the content, structure, and length of the report; (ii) To highlight key points to determine the purpose and central theme of the report; (iii) To review the research and determine the key ideas or concepts; and, (iv) To group ideas in a logical fashion and prepare a point form outline. Edit the outline to eliminate secondary or minor points.
5	A good executive summary should place emphasis on summarizing the following four major points: (i) One major conclusions or analysis; (ii) One major recommendation or decision; (iii) Something about the problem and what was studied; (iv) One major consideration.

6   The first sentence must grab and keep the reader. Authors should strive to grab the reader to peruse the entire executive summary. Avoid a dull start that easily puts off the readers. For instance, avoid the following approaches:
    (i) The purpose of the report ...;
    (ii) The problem question ...
7   As a cover sheet to a document, an executive summary should mention how the analysis was conducted, or on what are the conclusions based. Instead, begin with a concise statement of the conclusions of the research in the paper that would normally be attached.
8   After beginning with a summary statement of the findings, the executive summary should go on to provide a specific recommendation for action geared toward the audience. Finally, it should provide an analysis and justification for the recommendation by referring to the information summarized.
9   The elements to be included in an executive summary and the amount of space to be give to each element depend on the purpose and nature of the original document. Therefore, only choose the elements that make sense for the document.
10 A good executive summary should briefly cover every main section vis a vis the Introduction (Issue, Purpose, Scope and Limitations, and Alternatives), Significant Considerations, and Analysis and Decisions.

The detailed writing should be as follows:

§	Rule description
1	In the executive summary, put the Issue (Problem) and Purpose in the first paragraph;
2	The Scope and Limitations, as well as the Alternatives (Procedures), will go in the next paragraphs.
3	The Significant Considerations, Analysis, and Decisions will comprise the final paragraphs. When writing the Considerations or Findings, concentrate on the major findings. Make sure to stress the results (i.e. data) without conclusions or generalizations.
4	When writing the Analysis or Conclusions, authors may concentrate on the generalizations.
5	Upon reaching the Decisions or Recommendations, talk about specifics. Tell the research direction or new avenues based on the data.

3.3. ORIGINAL RESEARCH ARTICLES

Original research reports are divided into short communication, also known as technical communication and research report. Short communication is a rapid way of communicating extra-ordinary new scientific findings of importance to the scientific community. As the name depicts, it is supposed to be short (not more than 4000 words). Commonly, but not always, sections in a manuscript of original research reports are organized in the following structure: Introduction, Methods, Results, and Discussion, which is usually referred by its abbreviation as the IMRAD structure. Where there are possible variation journals, book editors or conference organizers may provide specific instructions for the authors.

3.3.1. Choosing the Title

The title should be concise and precise. It should summarize the main idea of the paper in 10-12 words. Make the title informative and descriptive of the work being reported. It should always avoid misleading the leader and being unrepresentative. Start with a keyword if possible, but avoid redundant words in the title (e.g. "An investigation of ...").

A rule of the thumb for a good title is that a title can be constructed based on [8, 22, 33, 49]:

§	Rule of the thumb
1	Reporting the results of an experiment, for instance, (Dependent Variable) as a Function of (Independent Variable)
	Example,
	(a) Relationship of uranium toxicity to Lemna gibba and phosphorus
2	The Effects of (Independent Variable) on (Dependent Variable)
	Example,
	The Effect of phosphorus on uranium toxicity to *Lemna gibba* G3
3	To use the main finding as the title.
	Example,
	Phosphates regulates uranium toxicity to *Lemna gibba* G3

3.3.2. Writing an Abstract

An abstract is a specific kind of summary included with various kinds of scientific publications. Its purpose is to provide a brief and comprehensive summary of the study. It is very important because it is the only part of a report or article that many people will read. There are many different ways to summarize a scientific article or other document. For instance, the title itself is sort of a one-line summary, and an outline is also a summary. An "executive summary" is often a statement of the basic idea in simple terms. A summary of a grant proposal should be in non-technical language for readers that are not scientists. However, an abstract has certain features that set it aside from these. It is always short, and it is always written as a single paragraph, despite the fact that structured abstracts are now common, based on the IMRAD structure of papers. With abstracts, the bottom line is brevity: They should be as short as possible and still include the important information [2, 8, 22, 32, 49].

An abstract is an ordinary part of a research article in a journal; only a small percentage of journals do not require them. Abstracts are also common in review articles [50]. It should include a brief description of the problem being investigated, the methods used, the results, and their implications.

The qualities of a good abstract are:

§	The Rules
1	It should be accurate – do not include information here that is not in the body of the manuscript;
2	It should be self-contained - spell out abbreviations;
3	It should be concise – it should usually have 120 to 250 words maximum. As part of being concise, use digits for all numbers, except when they begin a sentence;
4	It should be specific – begin this section with the most important information and limit it to the four or five most important concepts, findings, or implications of the study;
5	It should not cite references;
6	It should use paraphrases rather than quotations; and
7	It should be in past tense for procedures and present tense for results.

The first step in writing the abstract is to identify the major point or points of the article. Sometimes it helps to make an outline, but that is not always necessary. When the main points have been written down, then find out what information is crucial to lead up to those points [1, 8, 14, 33, 49]. The research methods might be important if they are new or unusual, but if they are standard, they only need to be referred to briefly. Next, write down the conclusions that are drawn from the main points. When all are done, the abstract should have the following properties:

	Properties
1	Introductory statement, including statement of the problem to be addressed (sometimes not needed)
2	Research methods (described at length, only if it is unusual)
3	Results or other main points (absolutely essential)
4	Concluding statement, telling what the results mean

3.3.3. Choosing Keywords

Keywords are used for the retrieval of the article from bibliographic databases. They are also used for the library catalogues. Hence, chose words that most represent the scientific field of research and specific areas in the field. Avoid repeating words that already appear in the title because the bibliographic databases are organized by either titles, authors, or the field of research, or specific research area.

3.3.4. Writing an Introduction

The "Introduction" and "Conclusion" sections are the hardest parts to write in a manuscript; hence, authors should plan to spend a lot of time on them. Many writers prefer to write their introductions last because it is too difficult to construct a balance of general context required for a good introduction before the whole paper is written [5, 9, 23]. Often it is easier to achieve this after having already worked through writing the entire manuscript. If one needs to write the introduction first to set the stage for ones own thinking, they should resist the temptation to perfect it. By the time the rest of the manuscript is finished, it will likely need substantial modification. The same concerns apply to conclusions, abstracts, and summaries. These components of the paper are most often what people will read, and authors must get the message across in as direct, crisp, and enticing a manner as possible [5, 9, 23].

The main purpose of the introduction section is to tell the reader why a particular study was performed. In other words, authors have to inform the reader of the research question and indicate why it is important, and how it is unique when compared to previous studies [8, 22, 33]. The introduction section should start out broad, and become more and more specific as it progresses towards the end. Sometimes it may be important to begin by defining any relevant terms in the documents, then authors should go on to review the relevant literature. However, special care should be taken to avoid an exhaustive and historical review [5, 9, 23]. At this point, authors should make a clear connection between previous research and the present work. Authors may choose to include any hypothesis, as well as the rationales for them. Usually, research papers with clear hypothesis are easily accepted for publication. The final paragraph usually contains a statement that clearly and explicitly states why the study was performed. A good rule of the thumb states that this section should contain an absolute minimum of four paragraphs: the general introduction, the literature review, the connection of the present study to the literature, and the explicit statement of purpose.

3.3.5. Writing Methods Section

The purpose of the methods section is to describe in detail how the study was performed. The aim is to provide enough information that can enable a third person's ability to replicate the study. This is important because it reduces doubts of validity of results, which surrounds some studies, and ability of others to verify the findings. Hence, the methods section should be as detailed as possible while at the same time, avoid unnecessary details (e.g. 50 mg of the uranium salts ($UO_2(NO_3)_2$) were take from a half-filled bottle with a spatula and dissolved in a 50 ml beaker).

For studies that used experiments, the methods section can be divided into subsections like materials, apparatus, design, procedure and of course data analysis. If not, authors should provide good, detailed information when writing. The order is arbitrary, but the most important is that the sub-sections should flow in compliment of the other.

For experiments carried out in the field, it is important (but not always) to define the study site's conditions and environment. This can also be a subsection. Field surveys in ecoscience usually involve sampling. They usually do not differ very much from field experiments or trials when reporting in the methods. For a field survey study in which the researchers simply ask a set of questions to participants, the design section is not necessary. The survey itself may be included as an appendix (these types of surveys are more common in social sciences than in natural sciences). However, it is not always necessary to divide the method sections into subsections, as the methods can logically be followed without problems without separation into subsection.

Materials

Materials are things used in the experiments. This sub-section is labelled depending on materials used in the study. For instance, if chemicals (e.g. uranium, or arsenic salt) are used, use the sub-heading "chemicals". If test organisms (e.g. *Lemna*, fluorescence bacteria, daphnia etc) are used, the appropriate term would be subjects, but the sub-heading may directly be "Test Organisms". If humans are used, use the term participants. Include any details that are relevant to the study. For example, when chemicals are part of material, it is better to indicate the level of purity (e.g. industrial grade, or analytical grade). For water, the water quality is important. For media, the constituents of the media should be thoroughly defined, including, where possible, the preparation procedure.

Apparatus

Apparatus sections should detail the equipment used in the study. It is generally recommended that any instrument that has been used in the study should be clearly documented by the type, model, and where the equipment was manufactured, as well as the place of manufacture. Usually, this should be in parenthesis (e.g. Uranium content in the media was determined using ICP-MS (PQ2+ Thermo, Cheshire, England, UK). Always give the dimensions (and perhaps other descriptive details) of any important items used in the study. Standard equipment such as furniture, stopwatches, pencils, and paper do not need to be mentioned unless they constitute an important roll in the whole study. In this case, they may be simply mentioned in passing as part of the procedure.

Be careful not to describe procedures in this sub-section. Authors should make clear what purpose the apparatus served, but should not give many details on the use of the apparatus at this point. One hint in this regard is to avoid using action verbs in this section [1, 7, 42, 43, 49].

Design

Research design is one of the most important parts of the research report because it is the main part that makes the results reported valid. In other words, the design of the experiments will tell whether the report is worth publishing and even reading. Poorly designed research works are not worth reading because the results may not reflect the real scientific process. This section should be well written, and researchers should consider how valid the experiments are statistically and logically when designing the studies. When writing this sub-section, describe the design and clearly spell out the independent and dependent variables. Indicate what the levels of the independent variables were, and whether the factor(s) were repeated, matched, or independent. Further, describe how the materials were assigned and any control procedures used.

Procedure

The procedure sub-section should carefully summarize each step in the execution of the study. It should indicate what a typical test, trial, or session involved. Any phases that the study had or any instructions that the subjects received should be described in detail, and clearly [1, 7, 42, 43, 49]. When referring to groups, try to use descriptive labels. For example, instead of saying treatment 1 or the experimental group, authors might say "the Uranium Exposed Treatment". Another technique is to use abbreviations that emphasize meanings. For example, "There were three treatments, including, the control group, which received 0 mg L^{-1} of Uranium (U0), a low dose group receiving 1 mg L^{-1} of uranium (U1), and a high dose group receiving 7 mg L^{-1} of uranium (U4).

Analysis

Significance of analysis also helps to evaluate the quality of the results in the research report. The method used to generate and process data, for instance, chemical analytics, calculations, models, and statistics should be detailed under this subsections. The procedure and the chosen modes should be clearly indicated. For instance, the data was subjected to ANOVA using SPSS version 11.5. Alternatively, it can state that "the chemical speciation were calculated using PhreeqC".

3.3.6. Writing the Results Section

Many scientists prefer combining the results and discussion sections. In doing so, they interpolate and discuss the results as they are presented in the documents. Whether separated or not, the principle in reporting the results and discussing them later is done as one. Hence, in this compilation, it has been preferred to separate the two, but that does not necessarily mean that those who combine the sections are wrong, it is only a matter of preference. Before starting to present the results in the manuscript, look carefully at the results – take a good hard look at all those numbers collected during the study. Think of different ways to summarize them (describe) and make sense out of them (analyse) [1, 7, 42, 43, 49]. Include only results, which are relevant to the question(s) posed in the introduction, irrespective of whether or not the results support the hypothesis.

This section is easier to write if authors first make tables or figures that they intend to use. First, give a general description of the finding, and then go into the details. When presenting the results of statistical tests, give descriptive statistics before the corresponding inferential statistics [5, 6, 10]. Thus, give means or percentages (perhaps referring to a table or figure) before talking about the results of any statistical tests, which were performed. When presenting means, it is reasonable to use one additional digit of accuracy than what is contained in the raw data. If the raw data consisted of whole numbers, then the means should contain one decimal place. When presenting nominal or ordinal data, give the percents rather than frequencies (since percents are independent of the sample size). The general format for presenting an inferential statistic is: degree of freedom (df) = value, probability = value. Note that exact p values are preferred. Also, if the computer output says the probability is 0.0000, then, report it as 0.001. (See appendix 3). Where possible, include some statistical estimate of effect size. When actually presenting the results, try to emphasize the meaning of the statistics. That is, what is being tested should be clearly described as well as what the significance means for the variables involved.

Do not discuss the implications of the results in this section. Do not talk about the meaning of the "p" level or the null hypothesis, or what chance factors have to do with it. Since authors are writing for the scientific community, they can assume the reader will have a working knowledge of statistics. If they are presenting a lot of material here, they may wish to employ subheadings, as is done in the methods section. These subheadings should have meaning and relevance to the data, and should help to organize the presentation of it. In other words, they should not be organized by the type of analysis employed, because the reader does not expect this. It is a good idea to precede the subheadings with a paragraph informing the reader of the logical organization of this section. In cases where the reader would expect something to be significant and it is not, the authors should address the issue. Authors should not provide raw data unless, for some reason, a single subject approach is required.

Statistical tests are based on probability and can be in error, therefore, they do not really prove anything. In this case, scientists can only use wording that implies causality instead of "prove", if they actually manipulated the independent variable (i.e., performed an experiment).

Examples:

1   Suppose a macrophyte *Lemna gibba* received a pollutant (while employing appropriate controls, procedures, etc.) and found a significant difference in growth rate (with the macrophytes under contaminant performing more poorly than when unpolluted). In this case, authors would be able to conclude that the pollutant caused the difference in growth ability; it impaired growth.

2   Suppose macrophyte *Lemna gibba* is sampled from two contaminated water reservoirs receiving arsenic in an abandoned uranium-mining site. The macrophyte samples are compared in terms of content of arsenic in the water (as determined from the results of a survey) with growth ability and found a correlation (greater arsenic concentration in the water went along with poorer growth performance). Since correlation does not say much about causality, they could only conclude that there is a relationship between contaminant and growth ability.

3.3.7. Presentation of Result in Tables and Figures

The purpose of tables and figures is to report data too numerous or complicated to be described adequately in the text, and to reveal trends or patterns in the data. They are most often used to present results, but may also be used to present other information, such as the design or a theoretical schema. Generally, tables and figures should be able to stand-alone. One should not read the whole manuscript to understand a table or figure. Hence, a few rules of thumb for a good quality presentation of tables and figures include the following:

§	Rule of the thumb
1	Tables and figures should not duplicate the same information, but can complement one another. Likewise, one should not repeat the data point values in a table or figure in the text of the manuscript;
2	All tables and figures must be referred and introduced in the text. Similarly, only tables and figures that contribute to the message should be included and referred to each figure in the text;
3	Limit the number of tables and figures to those that provide essential information that cannot adequately be presented in the text;
4	Table and figures should be understandable on their own without reference to the text;

5	The tables and figure should be organized be numbered in the order of their reference in the text and in order they tell a story;
6	Tables and figures should be numbered separately;
7	There should be neither page breaks in the middle of a table or figure, nor text around; and,
8	The table titles and figure legends should be written in the past tense, and they may be limited to providing information regarding what the table or figure presented, but not a summary or interpretation of the results.

(i) Specifics on Figures[1]

Figures provide visual impact and therefore, they are often the best way to communicate the primary findings. They are traditionally used to display trends and group results, but can also be used effectively to communicate processes or to simply display detailed data [41]. The rule of the thumb of quality presentation and design of figures include the following:

§	Rule of the thumb
1	Figure caption or legends should include sufficient information to make the figure self-explanatory (without reference to the text). All abbreviations, symbols, and shading should be explained;
2	Do not put the figure caption on the figure;
3	Figures other than pictures should be presented in black and white for easy reproduction. Further, colour is extremely expensive to publish, and should only be used when it provides unique information;
4	If the figure is a chart or graph, verbally label the axes and provide a key if necessary. The label of each axis should include units of measurement and clearly identify the data being displayed (e.g. labelling each line in a graph);
5	Experimental details should be excluded from the legend; these details should be included in the methods section;
6	Photographs of subjects should be used only if written, informed consent was obtained prior to the taking of the photograph;
7	The rules on the choice of correct figure format include the following:
	a If independent and dependent variables are numeric, the most appropriate figure is line diagrams or scatter grams;
	b If only the dependent variable is numeric, the most appropriate figure

---

[1] The term "figure" technically include graphs, charts, photographs, micrographs, maps, electrophoretograms, polygraph recordings (e.g. ECG, EEG), and line drawings.

is bar graphs; and

c   For showing proportions, the most appropriate figures are bar graphs
     or pie charts

(ii) Specifics on Tables

Tables are used to make an article more readable by removing numeric data
from the text. Tables can also be used to synthesise existing literature, to explain
variables, or to present the wording of survey questions; however, unnecessary
tables should not be included in the manuscripts. Each table should be referred to
in the text. There are different ways to format tables. Most scientists prefer a
style of tables that do not contain any vertical lines; however, the format provided
by the publisher is most important and should be observed. General rules of the
thumb to be observed when creating figures are:

§	Rule of the thumb
1	Check with the journal, but most journals want the table title and table on the same page, with each table on a separate page in numerical order;
2	Use column headings and table notes accurately to simplify and clarify the table. In most cases, the meaning of each column should be apparent without reference to the text;
3	Usually, there are no periods used after the table number or title; and,
4	When using columns with decimal numbers, make the decimal points line up.

3.3.8. Writing the Discussion

The purpose of the results section is to evaluate and interpret the results,
especially with respect to the original research question. Many novice writers
begin their discussion section with a statement about problems with their methods
or the items in their results, about which they feel most insecure [5, 6, 10]. Begin
a discussion with a short restatement of the most important points from the results.
Start with a brief, non-technical summary of the results. In other words, tell the
reader about the main findings without using statistical terminology. These should
be what can be said clearly based on what was done, not what cannot be said or
what was not really done. Then, go on to discuss the implications of the results.
In other words, whatever found, it needs to be discussed. Use this statement to set
up the ideas to focus on in interpreting the results and relating them to the

literature. Emphasize any theoretical consequences of the results. Use sub-headings that structure the discussion around the ideas [5, 9, 23].

Authors may or may not also mention any limitations of the study and any suggestions for future research in this section. Finally, an ending paragraph should make a final summary statement of the conclusions drawn. Authors are, at this point, also encouraged, when appropriate, to comment on the importance and relevance of their findings – the relation of the findings related to the big picture. Some scientific writing guides prescribe that this section should contain an absolute minimum of three paragraphs: the non-technical summary, discussion of the results and their implications, and the concluding paragraph.

3.3.9. Writing the Conclusions

A conclusion differs from an abstract in that it is a summary of the research findings, and not the whole research work, as the abstract is. Conclusions are based on the evidence that was presented in the paper. One of the worst mistakes a writer can make is to end a paper without a conclusion, because what one writes in the conclusion is what the readers will remember most. If one just stops, the readers will remember nothing about what they have read. Some authors prefer not to write this as a section, but to include it in the discussion's last paragraphs. If the manuscript has a conclusions section, do not repeat the discussion points. In the conclusion, writers move their reader's focus outward from the detailed discussion in the body of the paper, and writers also bring the paper to a close. If the manuscript has not already explained plans for future work in the discussion section, do so in the conclusion, identifying gaps in the already reported study and how such gaps can be filled.

3.3.10. Reference Section

References contain any citations made in the manuscript and vice versa. If something is not cited in the text, then it should not appear in the reference section. This is where the reference section differences from a bibliography. Scientific papers should contain references and not bibliographies because the later is a compilation of any literature that may have contributed knowledge to a manuscript without necessarily being directly cited. Bibliographies are most often used in book sections or books, and sometimes in scientific reviews, The main aim of the reference section is to tell the readers where they can find citations in the paper.

3.3.11. Citation and Reference Section

Citation practices vary considerably in different types of writing. Most academic and professional writing requires a full citation, either in text or in a combination of a parenthetical citation in the text and a complete bibliography[11, 13, 15, 16]. When citing a reference, focus on the ideas, not the authors, unless the person who reported a result is an important point in a statement. However, the identity of the authors may be sometimes important to the meaning of a statement, in which case, emphasis on the citation is appropriate.

Examples of citations in the text:
(i)   Citing a single author
    (a) Uptake of arsenic by Lemna gibba is negatively affected by increasing concentration of phosphate (Mkandawire, 2004).
    (b) Mkandawire (2004) noted that uptake of arsenic by Lemna gibba was negatively affected by increasing concentration of phosphate.
    (c) In 2004, Mkandawire reported that uptake of arsenic by *Lemna gibba* was negatively affected by increasing concentration of phosphate.
(ii) Citing multiple authors
    For articles with two authors, spell both last names and present as above. With articles that have three or more authors, use the Latin abbreviation "et al.," which stands for "and others".
Examples:
    (a) Two authors
        Uptake of arsenic by *Lemna gibba* is negatively affected by increasing concentration of phosphate (Mkandawire and Dudel, 2004).
    (b) Three or more authors
        Uptake of arsenic by *Lemna gibba* is negatively affected by increasing concentration of phosphate (Mkandawire, et al., 2004).
(iii) Multiple citations in parentheses are placed alphabetically or chronologically, and they are separated by a semicolon and a space. Choice of which to use is usually specified by the respective journals.

Examples:
  (a) *Alphabetically*
      Uranium and arsenic speciation induce exudation in some aquatic
      macrophytes (Dudel, et al., 2003; Mkandawire and Dudel, 2002;
      Weiske, et al., 2005).
  (b) *Chronologically*
      Uranium and arsenic speciation induce exudation in some aquatic
      macrophytes (Weiske, et al., 2005; Dudel, et al., 2003; Mkandawire
      and Dudel, 2002).
(iv) Citing secondary information
      When citing second hand information, authors must be indicated
      clearly. Note that in this example, only "Mkandawire, et al." would be
      placed in the reference section.
Example:
  (a) Phosphate inhibits only arsenate uptake but not arsenate (Lyubun, et
      al., 2002 cited in Mkandawire, et al., 2004).

Note:
(i)   Citation can also be in form of a number in square parenthesis, like "[1]",
      where the number corresponds to full citation details in the bibliography.
      The arrangement of the bibliography in this case may be according to
      appearance in the document, or alphabetical order. For instance examples
      1(a), 3(a) and (b), and 4 would be:
      1(a)   Uptake of arsenic by *Lemna gibba* is negatively affected by
                  increasing concentration of phosphate [1].
      3(a) & (b) Uranium and arsenic speciation induce exudation in some
                  aquatic macrophytes [1,2,3].
      4   Phosphate inhibits only arsenate uptake but not arsenite
                  (Lyubun, et al., 2002 cited in [1]).
(ii) Depending on the journal, authors may be required to cite all authors
      when citing for the first time, and later as an abbreviation. For instance,
      example 2 (b) would be:
      (a) Uptake of arsenic by *Lemna gibba* is negatively affected by
          increasing concentration of phosphate (Mkandawire, Taubert and
          Dudel, 2004).

3.3.12. Writing the Acknowledgment Section

This section is optional. When authors decide to include it, the standard is to place it between the conclusion and reference sections. Acknowledgment should be included to accredit any significant help in thinking up, designing, or carrying out the work, or received materials from someone not part of the authorship. Authors must acknowledge assistance and the service or material provided, and any sources of funding that supported the research. Authors can acknowledge outside reviewers only if they reviewed the manuscript prior to evaluation. Although the acknowledgement must conform to usual style requirements of the whole manuscript, first person is preferred by many authors. Acknowledgments are always brief and never flowery [8, 22, 33].

3.4. RESEARCH REVIEWS ARTICLE

This type of manuscript does not follow the standard format that a research report does. Instead of the Introduction, Methods, Results, and Discussion sections, there is an Introduction, Body, and Conclusions, known as the IBAC structure. There are a number of kinds of research reviews. Some reviews describe a phenomenon, while others review an existing theory or present a new one [1]. The authors could critically evaluate how one theory accounts for some data as compared to some other theory.

3.4.1. Writing an Abstract of a Review Article

An abstract for a research review should include the topic and purpose, the scope of the material covered, the sources used and the conclusions. General preparation of the abstract and structure should follow that of the research report

3.4.2. Writing an Introduction of a Review Article

For most reviews, it is common that the section titled "Introduction" is never written or typed. This section is not unlike the introduction for a research report. Generally, the introduction should clearly define the problem or issue. It starts out broad and becomes more and more specific. It is often useful to use headings (and perhaps subheadings) in the body of the research report to help communicate the outline and organization of the paper to the reader [1, 8, 22, 33]. Therefore, at the end of the introduction, just before the actual body of the paper, there should appear a paragraph that lets the reader know the direction that the paper will take. It is a good idea to precede the headings with a paragraph informing the reader of the logical organization (i.e., other headings that will be employed).

3.4.3. Writing the Body

The "Body" section does not bare the heading name. It is silent because it is present in form of specific discussion sub-sections that cumulatively makes the body section. If headings are used, the primary main heading levels should be treated like the main heading of a research report. All levels of headings should be clearly differentiated. For instant, the authors may choose to flush left and italicise second level headings. This section can be lengthy, depending upon how much material is presented. It should present the relevant literature and ideas. To write this perfectly, authors should set themselves a minimum number of references that are required. These references should be listed in the reference section and should be cited using a particular style, which they can be seen most clearly in the literature. A common mistake is often to organize the paper around the specific references being used, where other writers even use the reference titles as the main headings of the manuscript [8, 22, 33]. The paper should be organized around the relevant phenomenon or theory and not by the specific references. The authors should try to identify relations, contradictions, gaps, and inconsistencies in the literature. They should also suggest possible solutions to any problem identified, and future directions for research to take.

3.4.4. Writing the Conclusions of a Review Article

Finally, there is always need of an ending section, in which, the main points made in the article are summarise. In all, it is not different from the conclusion in the scientific report.

3.5. PREREQUISITE TO SUBMISSION OF A MANUSCRIPT

Before submitting a manuscript to the targeted journal, authors should take a break for a few days after writing before checking. They should also make sure not to rely on spelling or grammar checkers. Make several passes to check general impressions – structure and suitability conformity with instructions to authors' requirements set aside by the targeted journal. Usually, authors may not manage to spot some simple mistakes like spellings, grammar, and typographic in their own documents. Here, a fresh eye would help to spot such mistakes – these fresh eyes are those from colleagues whom authors should ask to check their manuscripts. Primary author's or guarantor's should take ultimate responsibility.

Once the paper is thoroughly checked, authors should question themselves before submission for publication consideration. Once the questions have been answered, the paper is ready for wider consumption. Before submission, the authors should make sure that the manuscript answers the questions in the checklist below:

---

1   Topic
   i.   Does the paper stick to the topic?
   ii.   Is there a clear definition of what the central topic or issue is?
   iii. Is the topic sufficiently narrowed or broadened such that it can be dealt with fully in the assigned length?
   iv.   Is there a clear rationale for analyzing or discussing this topic?
   v.   Is there a clear thesis or perspective on the topic: not just "what," but "what about it?"

2   Ideas
   i.   Are the ideas too general, too descriptive, and too full of generalizations that they cannot be supported? Are the ideas clinched, or repetitious?
   ii.   Are there potential problematic or controversial elements? Are there potential objections or alternate approaches?
   iii. Does the argument made in the body lead logically and inevitably to the conclusion(s)?
   iv.   Is there a good balance between ideas and evidence?

3   Organization and Structure
   i.   Are the sections of the paper clearly defined and are headings used correctly?
   ii.   Does the introduction define the issue, state a rationale, and indicate

---

a focus for your discussion/analysis?

iii.   Does each paragraph in the body address a distinct idea or contribute to the development of a distinct idea of its section?

iv.   Does the conclusion merely restate the topic or thesis, or does it offer a genuine conclusion?

v.   The three principles of effective organization: Does the paper, as a whole, each section, each paragraph, and each sentence, have unity (deals with one idea), coherence (moves smoothly and logically), and emphasis (important points strategically placed)?

4   Expression

i.   Is the writing style concise, direct, and interesting?

ii.   Is the diction appropriate: good, varied vocabulary; precision in word choice; clear, simple over long, and Latinate (e.g., "walk" vs. "achieve an ambulatory state")?

iii.   Are there errors in mechanics: grammar, punctuation, usage, and spelling?

iv.   Are the citations, referencing, and formatting complete and accurate?

3.6. RESPONDING TO REVIEWERS AND EDITORS CRITICISM

Once a manuscript is submitted, the editor evaluates the suitability of the manuscript to the scope of the journal before a review process commences. If the manuscript is out of scope, the editor immediately returns the paper to the author. If the editor believes that the subject of the paper falls outside the scope of the journal, there is no point in challenging this. There is no choice but to submit the manuscript to another journal.

Once the review processes commences and the reviewers have done their work, the journal's editor sends a notice to the authors containing comments from the different reviewers, whose identities are normally kept confidential. Upon the recommendations of the reviewers and the editor's assessment, the notification may either reject or provisionally accept the manuscript.

If the editor has rejected the manuscript, there are usually reasons given for the decision. Then, authors need to assess the reviewers' comments to determine whether the manuscript can be accepted after certain revisions are made. In most cases, the editors and reviewers try to help the authors to produce a high quality manuscript. In whatever case, the authors should not take the reviewers' comments personally. In some instances, it might be bad timing because the journal might have just accepted or published a similar study. One can always submit the manuscript to another journal. It is usually best to consider the reviewers' comments when revising the manuscripts, even when the authors feel that the reviewers have misunderstood the paper, because others may do the same.

If the manuscript has been provisionally accepted, the authors should plan a strategy for revising the paper and gaining full acceptance. This includes resubmitting a fully revised manuscript and responses to the reviewers' comments. It is advisable not to add new sections unless requested to do so; otherwise, any new section added may initiate the whole review process once more.

The following can serve as a rule of the thumb when responding to the reviewers' comments and resubmitting the manuscript [51]:

§	Rule of the thumb
1	Read all of the comments from reviewers and the editor.
2	Never respond immediately, but allow a few days to reflect on the comments,
3	If the comments from the editor and reviewers can be used to improve your manuscript, by all means, make those changes.
4	If the manuscript has been rejected and authors still feel that the work deserves publication, send it quickly to another journal[2]. Some data can become less relevant when too much time passes.
5	If the manuscript has been provisionally accepted, it should be responded to promptly. As soon as possible, begin drafting a polite, thoughtful, clear, and detailed response.
6	Avoid a defensive or confrontational tone in the response. The goal is to extract helpful information from the comments, adopt any useful suggestions to improve the manuscript, and calmly explain the point of view when the authors disagree.
7	Authors should respond completely to each comment in an orderly, itemized manner, and if necessary, copy and paste into the letter any substantive changes made to the manuscript. There is no limit on the length of your response. Most editors are willing to read a long and complete response.
8	Change and modify the manuscript where it makes sense. Authors are not required to make every suggested change, but they need to address all of the comments. If they reject a suggestion, the editor will want a good

---

[2] I have the experience of the same manuscript being rejected in a low impact journal and accepted in a very high impact journal after very minor revisions

reason with evidence supported by references.

9   Reviewers do not always agree with each other, in which case the authors must make a choice on whose recommendations seem more valid because the know the research best. In a response letter to the editor, the authors should state that they received conflicting advice and made what they think is the best choice.

10   If the reviewers is obviously wrong or they have misunderstood, authors are entitled to provide an argument and provide facts that can be referenced.

11   Comments made in the response letter should match the revisions in the manuscript. Otherwise, the editors become irritated when they find mismatches.

3.7. CHAPTER COMPENDIUM

The process of getting a paper published in a scientific peer-reviewed journal is a challenging, but rewarding one, once all the hard work finally pays off and the reprints arrive. Writing an effective scientific paper is not easy. A good rule of thumb is to write as if a person who knows about the field in general, but does not already know what was done in the study, will read the paper. Before embarking on writing a scientific paper, it is advisable to read some scientific papers that have been written in the same format of the planned paper. In addition to the science, a lot of attention should be paid to the writing style and format.

Therefore, the chapter just finished covered how to start, what to write, how to structure the sentences and paragraphs, and how to improve the writing style. Then, it talks about designing the document for different audiences and different purposes. It reviews the standard scientific reporting framework and discusses how it can be tailored to the needs of both the writer and their audience.

Chapter 4

HOW TO CLEAR THE FOG FROM SCIENTIFIC WRITING?

During a foggy day, the visibility depends on the thickness of the fog – the thicker the fog, the shorter the distance one can see. This has been analogized to readability of a writing work. A work that is difficult to read is said to contain fog; thus, readability of a work depends on thickness of the fog it contains [52]. There are many possible forms of quantitative representation of readability[1]. They are mostly based on the belief that the longer the sentences and the more complicated the words, then the more difficult it is to read the text. A simple scale based on these factors is provided by the Fog Index[2] [53].

Unfortunately, science is often hard to read [47]. Most people assume that the difficulties are born out of necessity due to the extreme complexity of scientific concepts, data, and analysis [47]. Further, most scientific writings pack technical detail so densely that even a most interested and informed reader may find it difficult to follow without re-reading. Despite that, they may be the source of the fog; some of the technical details seem inevitable, for instance, scientific terms,

---

[1] Since the late 1940s, reading specialists have created several objective measurements of readability. The most frequently used measurements are (1) the Flesch Reading Ease Scale (Flesch 1948), (2) the Gunning Fog Index (Gunning 1968) and Fry's Index (Fry 1977).

[2] To determine the fog index, representative samples of around a hundred words long are selected from throughout the text being studied. From these the average sentence length and the percentage of words containing three or more syllables are determined. The Fog Index measures the grade level of a piece of writing (i.e., assumed readability) by manipulating two factors: the average sentence length and the percentage of hard words. The larger the numerical value of the index, the harder the text is to read. Applying the test to a range of papers in current scientific journals produces a Fog index of about 19, which implies that those scientific papers are very difficult to read than articles in newspapers.

jargons, and formulas in chemistry, physics, biology, and mathematics, just to mention a few. How can scientific writers soften the impact of all the specialized jargon, mathematical formulas, technical, and scientific terms that seem so essential in technical papers? Writing style and use of words are major sources of the fog in scientific writing. Again, how can novice and ESL scientist write with less, or without any fog? This is the objective of this chapter, to provide relatively easy ways to reduce and eliminate the fog in scientific writing. This chapter tries to provide a means of breaking up and expanding technical terms to decrease their density and to eliminate as many technical terms as possible by replacing them with everyday equivalents. Furthermore, it provides a tool in writing style that either eliminates or reduces the fog in scientific papers.

4.1. REAL FOG IN SCIENTIFIC WRITING

Readability cannot be contained within the narrow limits of sentence length and long words. For instance, short and choppy sentences are often harder to follow than a smooth, longer sentence with adequate transitions. Familiarity with the subject matter and the ease of following organizational patterns are more important than more easily quantifiable properties. However, passive and negative constructions, long noun strings, dangling modifiers, nominalizations, poor punctuation, and the mixing of different English varieties interfere more with readability than do long words by themselves. Furthermore, many technical terms make a passage more difficult and harder to understand. Consequently, it becomes difficult to hold a reader's interest.

4.2. CLEARING THE FOG OF VOCABULARY AND TECHNICAL TERMS

A text is clear and readable when special words aimed to make the writing look more technical, scientific, or academic are avoided where the message can be more clearly presented in everyday language. However, it should be taken into consideration that every scientific field has special terms that cannot be avoided. For instance, terms used in chemistry can sometimes cause fog when read by biologist, geologists, or physicists. Mathematical, chemical, or physics formulas have no replacement, but, what should be avoided are writings aimed at trying to impress readers by using words most people have never heard or can not understand [8, 17, 22, 33]. It is important to use words that most people would understand without using the dictionary. Thus, colloquial language[3] , slang, or contraction words, or phrases should be avoided where possible. As a rule in scientific writing, never use contractions.

Examples:

Unacceptable	Acceptable	Remarks
it's	it is	Contractions
can't	cannot	"can not" is also wrong
don't	do not	Contractions
wouldn't	-would not	Contractions
couldn't	Could not	Contractions
haven't	Have not	Contractions
I'm	I am	Contractions
wanna	Want to	Colloquialisms
gonna	going to	Colloquialisms

4.3. CLEARING THE FOG OF JARGON[4]

Use of jargon, where regular language would do, spoils the communication in most scientific works [18]. The term "jargon" has several meanings, but in a broad sense, it denotes the writer's preference for "woolly" words, phrases, and grammatical constructions [54]. The sources of and remedies for jargon in learned science have been thoroughly discussed in numerous publications [55]. Here, the foci are on "eco-speak"- the jargonistic variety of the English of environmental professionals [56]. In particular, it contains a list of words that keep coming up as sources of needless complexity in ecoscience reporting.

---

[3] A colloquialism, which is referred to collectively as colloquial language, are expressions not used in formal speech, writing, or paralinguistics. Colloquialisms or colloquial language are only appropriate for casual, ordinary, familiar, or informal conversation rather than formal speech or scientific writing.

[4] A summarised version of the jargons section was published as D.N. Tychinin, M. Mkandawire, English for Ecoscience: A Miniguide for Ex-Soviet and Eastern European Contributors, Environ. Sci. Pollut. Res. 11(2004) 67.

Examples:

Jargon	How to avoid them
Anthropogenic or **anthropic** (adj.)	As in *anthropogenic chemicals* or *anthropic soils.* Although anthropogenic is an established "term of the environment", it is overused in the sense of "man-made" or "human-caused".
Apply (v.)	As in water was applied by sprinkling (= water was sprinkled).
Approach (n.)	As in *in a phased approach* (= by phases), *conservative in approach* (= conservative), or *the toxicity assessment approach* (= toxicity assessment).
Base (*n.*)	As in *our scientific information base.* Could we switch from that computer speak to something direct, e.g., "the information we collected"?
Circumstances (*n. pl.*)	As in some circumstances (= sometimes).
Conditions (*n. pl.*)	As in observed under serum bottle conditions (= observed in serum bottles).
Cost-effective or **cost-efficient** (*adj.*)	Instead of economical or profitable, as in a cost-efficient technical-administrative set of tools for optimized investigation.
Current(ly) (*adj.* and *adv.*)	As in *the current authors* (= we), or *currently under way* (= under way).
Different (*adj.*)	As in different alternatives. Are there "identical alternatives"?
Factor (*n.*)	As in *site factors* (= soil, groundwater, etc.). "The word is overused as a blanket term when more precise alternatives such as *component, element, occurrence, feature,* or *consideration* are available ....".
Following (*prep.*)	As in *following the procedures of* (= after) [Author, et al.]. Here, following means "in the style of", but its use as a synonym for *after* in the sense "later than" is also discouraged [54, 55].
Form (*n.*)	As in was in a bioavailable form (= was bioavailable).
Level (*n.*)	As in *have a low level of quality* (= be of low quality), or *at the national level* (= nationally). Avoid using "level" to mean "concentration" or

	"content."
Manner (n.)	As in *in a consistent manner* (= consistently), *in the most time-effective manner possible* (= promptly), or *drilled in a manner to maximize* (= drilled to maximize). See also Day (1998). Manner is probably the number one language-pollutant in the environmental sciences.
Nature (*n.*)	As in *waste of a municipal nature* (= municipal waste), or *specialized in its nature* (= specialized).
Part (n.)	As in an essential part of (= essential for).
Practically (adv.)	As in *practically impossible*. Is it *almost* impossible, or is it impossible *from the practical point of view*?
Remove (v.)	As in *removed by dredging* (= dredged away/out), or *removed by washing* (= washed off).
Scale (*n.*)	as in *increased on a worldwide scale* (= increased worldwide).
Stage (*n.*) or **step** (*n.*)	As in *losses during purification stages* (= losses during purification) or *a cryofocusing step of the sample* (= cryofocusing of the sample).
Supernatant or **supernate** (*n.*)	As in supernatant samples (= supernatant-liquid samples).
Target (n.)	As in *much more data is needed to reach this target* (= goal). I also recall having seen the obscure *environmental targets* used to mean "natural-protection tasks" in one article, and "objects of study" in another.
Tool (n.)	As in an effective tool for (= effective in).
Virtually (adj.)	As in virtually (= nearly) complete.
Volume (n.)	As in a small volume of (= a little) acidified water.
Way (n.)	As in in an efficient way (= efficiently).

4.4. CLEARING OF THE FOG OF MODIFIERS

Most manuscripts I have reviewed or proofread have problems in the correct use of modifiers, regardless of whether the contributor or writer is a native English speaker or ESL speaker. However, German contributors may easily place dangling modifiers because of the German grammar, where verbs are always placed at the end of the sentence. Thus, I would like to discuss modifiers in a bit of detail.

A modifier is a descriptive word or group of words giving important information about another word or group of words in a sentence. A modifier describes, clarifies, or gives more detail about a concept, or the other word or words. In a way, a modifier logically attaches itself to the word or words it is modifying. A writer can confuse a reader by misplacing a modifier in a sentence. Thus, it is important to be sure where to place modifiers in sentences so that a reader will be certain of the word or words they modify, on one had, while on the other, reduce confusion or awkward statements.

4.4.1. Dangling Modifier

A dangling modifier is a word, phrase, or clause that modifies a word not clearly stated in the sentence [57]. Dangling modifiers have no referent in the sentence. The meaning of the sentence, therefore, is left dangling. For instance, consider the statement below:

Flowing into the tailing pond, the uranium increased two-folds in the water.

In the example, the uranium did not flow the tailing pond, the tailing water did. To be technical, the first part is the "dependent clause", and it must have the same subject as the "independent clause" which follows. From this example, it is clear that dangling modifiers frequently lead to confusion that may result in a readers misunderstanding the content of manuscripts. Therefore, here are some sources of dangling modifiers in scientific writing for environmental sciences, and how to avoid them, most of the examples have been adapted from Dolainski [58]:

i.   Dangling Modifiers Due to Use of Passive Voice:
      Many of dangling modifiers result from use of the passive voice. Such dangling modifiers can be avoided by simply writing in the active voice.

Example 1:

Dangling	After sequentially extracting the sediment sample into fractions, organic-bound arsenic was measured.
Correct	After sequential extracting of the sediment sample into fractions,

	we measured the fraction of organic-bound arsenic.
Remark	We, not organic-bound arsenic, sequentially extracted the sample into fractions.

Example 2:

Dangling	The arsenic speciation was determined using this procedure.
Correct	Using this procedure, I determined the speciation.
Remark	I, not the arsenic speciation, used the procedure.

Example 3 (unknown source):

Dangling:	To test this hypothesis, the participants were divided into two groups.
Correct:	To test this hypothesis, we divided the participants into two groups.
Remark	We, not the participants, tested the hypothesis.

ii.   Dangling Participial Phrases:

A participle is a word that ends in "ing" or "ed" and looks like a verb; yet, it is not actually an adjective that modifies a specific noun or pronoun. If it does not, then it is a dangling participle. The most common forms of dangling participles are caused by failing to observe the following three rules of thumb:

§	Rule of the thumb
1	The participle should be placed closed to the word to which it refers, and there should be no intervening noun to which the participle might seem to refer.
2	A participle at the beginning of a sentence (or at the beginning of a second independent clause in a compound sentence) should refer to the subject of the sentence of the independent clause.
3	A participle following the main clause should refer to a definite noun, not to the general thought expressed by the clause.
4	Sometimes changing the sentence from the passive to the active voice corrects the modification problem of dangling participial phrases.
5	Transform the participial phrase into an independent clause to emphasise an idea and to get rid of the dangling modifier.

Example 1:

Dangling	Adding PO_4^{3-}, the arsenate uptake by the plant decreased.
Correct	As we added PO_4^{3-}, the arsenate uptake by the plant decreased. *or* Adding PO_4^{3-}, we noticed the decrease uptake of arsenate by the plant.
Remark	The placement of the participial phrase "Adding PO_4^{3-}" implies that the arsenic uptakes by the plants were adding the PO_4^{3-}.

Example 2:

Dangling	These HeLa cells[5] disappeared from the sterile hood, thus causing us very much worry.
Correct	Because the HeLa cells disappeared from the sterile hood, we are very worried.
Remark	Instead of modifying a particular word, "causing" modifies the entire clause that appears before the comma.

   iii. Dangling Gerund Phrases:

A dangling gerund phrase can be corrected by adding a noun or a pronoun in order to modify it.

Example:

Dangling	After analyzing with ACP-MS, the uranium decreased.
Correct	After analysing with ICP-MS, we observed that the uranium concentration had decreased.
Remark	Since there is no other noun phrase for it to modify, the gerund "looking" appears to modify "storm."

   iv. Dangling Infinitive Phrases:

An infinitive phrase must modify the noun performing the action. When a phrase is placed wrongly or far way from the noun, the infinitive phrases are also commonly left dangling. To correct the problem, here are the rules of the thumb:

---

[5] A HeLa cells are immortal cell lines used in molecular biology and medical research. The cell lines were derived from cervical cancerous cells taken from Henrietta Lacks, who died from cancer on 4th October 1951.

§   Rule of the thumb

1   Do not split infinitives awkwardly.

2   Change the sentence to active voice.

3   Avoid separating a subject from its predicate, a verb from its object, or the parts of a verb phrase.

Example:

Dangling	To analyze uranium in groundwater samples, ICP-MS and right calibration standards are needed.
Correct	To analyze uranium in groundwater samples, one will need ICP-MS and right calibration standards. or If one wants to analyze uranium in groundwater, one needs ICP-MS and right calibration standards.
Remark	There is no one in the above sentence who will analyze the groundwater sample.

v.   Elliptical Clauses:

An elliptical clause has the subject or verb implied rather than stated. The subject of the clause has to be the same as the subject of the main clause, otherwise it is dangling.

Example:

Dangling	While determining phenol concentration in the groundwater samples, the UV-vis spectroscope broke down.
Correct	While we were determining phenol concentration in the groundwater samples, our UV-vis spectroscope broke down. *or*: While determining phenol concentration in the ground water samples, we broke down our UV-vis spectroscope.

vi.   Dangling Modifiers at the Beginning of a Sentence

Dangling modifiers frequently appear at the beginning of a sentence as a group of words used to introduce the sentence. Mostly, the phrase begins with an *–ed* or *–ing* word, or words like although, before, in, to, when, while, or with.

Example 1 (unknown source):

Dangling:	Working overtime, the project was finished by the deadline.
Correct:	Working overtime, we finished the project by the deadline.
Remark	The project did not work overtime.

Example 2 (unknown source):

Dangling	Before he became ill, my father's life was comfortable and satisfying.
Correct	Before he became ill, my father enjoyed a comfortable, satisfying life.
Remark	My father, not his life, became ill.

viii. Dangling Modifier at the End of a Sentence:
A dangling modifier can also pop up at the end of a sentence.

Example 1:

Dangling	The transfection of nanodiamond immunoconjugates became very visible viewing on the fluorescence microscope.
Correct	The transfection of nanodiamond immunoconjugatess became very visible as we viewed with fluorescence microscope.
Remark	The transfection of nanodiamond immunoconjugates was not viewing.

Example 2 (unknown source):

Dangling	The test was difficult, not having studied enough.
Correct	The test was difficult for me because I did not study enough.
Remark:	The test did not study.

4.4.2. Misplaced Modifiers

There is a certain degree of freedom in deciding where to place a modifier in a sentence [59]. The modifier can be placed at the end, immediately after the subject or as an introductory phrase just before the subject.

Example:
1   We stirred the samples vigorously.

2   We vigorously stirred the samples.

3   Vigorously, we stirred the samples.

However, this freedom of where to place the modifier sometimes leads to confusion in the sentence when a modifier is misplaced. Modifiers, positioned wrongly, may modify the wrong thing.

i.   Misplaced Words:
      In general, single-word modifiers should be placed near the word or words they modify. Otherwise, a reader may think that they modify something different in the sentence. Below are examples of where a modifier is misplaced and how the confusion can be eliminated.

Example:

Confusing	We could detect the spectrum of MTBE dissolved in the groundwater easily.
Correct	We could easily detect the spectrum of MTBE dissolved in groundwater.
Remark	Do we detect the spectrum easily, or do the MTBE dissolve easily?

ii.   Misplaced Prepositional Phrase and Dependent Clause:
      Similar to single word modifiers, it is equally important to place modifying phrases or clauses as close as possible to the word or words they modify.

Example 1:

Confusing	They removed the uranium using biosorption in the mine water.
Correct	They removed the uranium in the mine using mine water.

Example 2:

Confusing	We heard that the safety manager intended to conduct a safety drill while we were in the biochemistry laboratory.
Correct	While we were in the biochemistry laboratory, we heard that the safety manager intended to conduct a safety drill.

Example 3:	
Confusing	After the successful conjugation experiments, Msau told us at her institute that she would start transfecting nanodiamonds into the HeLa cells.
Clear	Msau told us at her institute that she would start transfecting nanodiamonds into the HeLa cells after the successful conjugation experiments.

iii. Misplaced Limiting Modifiers:

Words that modify expressions immediately following them are limiting modifiers (e.g. almost, even, hardly, just, merely, nearly, not, only, nearly, just, simply, etc). Placement of the limiting modifiers in a sentence has a very important impact on the meaning of the sentence. They should always go immediately before the word or words they modify otherwise the sentence becomes confusing. Many writers regularly misplace these modifiers.

Example 1 (unknown source):	
Confusing	Ibrahim has nearly annoyed every professor he has had.
Clear	Ibrahim has annoyed nearly every professor he has had.
Remark	The former means the person did not do it, while the latter means he did it

Example 2:	
Confusing	We almost used all of the biomarkers in the experiment.
Correct	We used almost all of the biomarkers in the experiment.

iv. Misplaced Lengthy Modifiers:

(a) Between subjects and predicates

Placing lengthy modifiers between the subject and the predicate of a sentence frequently results into awkward statements, therefore, the placement of modifiers between the subject and predicate should be limited to only short ones.

Example:	
Awkward	The need for remediation in abandoned uranium mining sites, because of stringent international and local directives on water quality, has risen sharply in recent years.

Correct	The need for remediation in abandoned uranium mining sites has risen sharply in recent years because of stringent international and local directives on water quality.

(b) Between a Verb and its Complement:
   It is advisable to limit single word modifiers between a verb and its complement. Placing a lengthy modifier between a verb and its complement should utmost be avoided.

Example:

Awkward	The chemistry award-winning student seemed, to the surprise of the lecturers, unsatisfied.
Clear	To the surprise of the lecturers, the chemistry award-winning student seemed unsatisfied.
	or
	The chemistry award-winning student seemed unsatisfied.

(c) Within a Verb Phrase:
   It is advisable to use a single word modifier within a verb phrase. Placing a lengthy modifier within a verb phrase should, at all costs, be avoided.

Example:

Awkward	The transfection of nanodiamond is, when modified by 4th generation dendrimer, mediated.
Common	The transfection of nanodiamond is mediated by modified 4th generation dendrimer.

4.4.3. Squinting Modifiers

A squinting modifier can seem to modify either the word preceding it or following it [59]. In other words, the modifier is "squinting" in both directions at the same time. The ambiguous result can confuse the reader.

Example 1:

Confusing	Defining the objectives clearly strengthens project justification.
Correct	Defining the objectives will clearly strengthen project

| | justification.
or
A clear definition of the project objectives strengthens project justification. |

Example 2:	
Confusing	A chemist who experiments occasionally gets correct results.
Clear	Occasionally, a chemist who experiments gets correct results.

4.4.4. Split Infinitives

Split infinitive is when a word or words are inserted between the "to" and the verb of an infinitive form [59]. Some regard a split infinitive as an error, while others accept split infinitives even in formal writing. Nevertheless, it is preferable to avoid splitting infinitives, especially when placing a long and disruptive modifiers between the "to" and the verb [60]. However, writers must use their own judgement when it comes to single-word modifiers. Sometimes a sentence becomes awkward if a single-word modifier is placed anywhere but between the elements of the infinitive.

Example:	
Wrong	The scientist decided to, before they conducting the MTBE biodegradation experiment, run a pre-experiment with the biocer.
Right	The scientist decided to run a pre-experiment with the biocer before they conducted the MTBE biodegradation experiment.

4.5. CLEARING THE FOG OF GENDER AND SEXISM[6]

Writing with gender biased can sometimes bring fog in writing because the readers may fail to concrete on the actual message in the text. Thus, gender free language is a requirement in scientific writing an all other activities of the academia because unbiased language lets readers to concentrate on what one says rather than how one says it [34]. It may be easy to avoid gender-biased, for instance, by replacing sexist nouns with more neutral ones.

---

[6] This section is based on an article by Sharon Cogdill and Judith Kilborn "Avoiding Gender Bias in Pronouns" on http://leo.stcloudstate.edu/style/genderbias.html

Examples:

Gender Biased	Gender Neutral
Chairman	Chair, or Chairperson
Man	Human
Congressman	Senator or Representative

In a number of instances, pronouns like *he*, *him*, and *his* are used when one refera to nouns meant to include both genders. Gender neutral, in such instances, can be achieved by the following five options (rules of the thumb):

§	Rule of the thumb

1   Using the plural form for both nouns and pronouns
    Examples:

    Biased   Studying the techniques by which a celebrated writer achieved his success can stimulate any writer faced with similar problems.

    Unbiased   Studying the techniques by which celebrated writers achieved their success can stimulate any writer faced with similar problems.

2   Omitting the pronoun altogether
    Examples:

    Biased   Each doctor should send one of his nurses to the workshop.

    Unbiased   Each doctor should send a nurse to the workshop.

3   Using "his or her", "he/she", or "s/he" when occasionally needed to stress the action of an individual is inevitable. Such references will not be awkward unless they are frequent, however, their use in scientific writing should be very limited
    Examples:

    Biased   If you use a technical term he may not understand, explain it.

    Unbiased   (i) If you use a technical term he or she may not understand, explain it.

                     (ii) If you use a technical term he/she may not understand, explain it.

4   Varying pronoun choice when emphasising an action of an individual. Ideally, choose pronouns that work to counter prevailing stereotypes.
    Examples:

    a. Biased   Gradually, toddlers will see the resemblance between block creations and objects in his world, and he will

		begin to name some structures, like "house," and "chimney."
	Unbiased	Gradually, toddlers will see the resemblance between block creations and objects in her world, and she will begin to name some structures, like "house," and "chimney."
b.	Biased	The kitchen can serve as a center for new experiences, an interesting place where important things happen, and where she has a chance to learn about the way big-people things are done.
	Unbiased	The kitchen can serve as a centre for new experiences, an interesting place where important things happen, and where he has a chance to learn about the way big-people things are done.

5   Switching from the third-person (he) to the second-person (you).
    Examples:

Biased	Each scientist should report his research progress to the supervisor before the year ends.
Unbiased	(i) You should report your research progress to the supervisor before the year ends.
	(ii) Report your research progress to the supervisor before the year ends.

4.6. CLEARING FOG OF ENGLISH VARIETIES[7]

One frequent mistake by most ESL writers is the inconsistent usage of one English variety, particularly between the American and British English. Many scientific writers, including journal editors and reviewers of ESL may not realize that the two English varieties have some major differences that once used interchangingly, may confuse the reader or may even cause a misunderstanding of the whole message being communicated. There are a few rules in determining the variety one is writing, although the rules may sometimes not apply. Hence, one has to learn to recognize the varieties without special rules.

---

[7] I decided to dwell on this area again because it is a major problem for most scientists regardless of EFL or ESL. For instance, a reviewer, probably more acquainted to the standard American English variety, wrote on a submission written in standard British English, "what type of scientists are these, inventing their own words. For example, 'characterisation', 'recognise' are non-English words. I recommend you (editor) don't publish a paper in this horrible state."

4.6.1. The Noun Endings

(a) *The "-our" vs. "-or"*

Generally, Americans use of *-or* as a word ending is equivalent to *-our* in British usage. Most words ending in unstressed *-our* in the British English end in *-or* in American English, except where the vowel is unreduced or unread.

Examples 1:

American	British
color	colour
flavor	flavour
honor	honour
armor	armour
rumor	rumour
neighbor	neighbour

Examples 1: Exception due to vowel is unreduced

American	British
contour	contour
paramour	paramour
troubadour	troubadour
endeavour	endeavour

(b) *The "-re" vs. the "-er"*

In British usage, some words end with a consonant followed by *-re*, with the *-re* unstressed. Most of these words have the ending *-er* in the American usages. The difference is most common for words ending *-bre* or *–tre*.

Examples:

American	British
center	centre
meter	metre
liter	litre
fiber	fibre
theater	theatre
goiter	goitre
saltpetre	saltpeter

However, the ending –*cre* is preserved in American English to indicate that the *c* is pronounced *k* rather than *s*.

Examples:

American	British
acre	Acre
lucre	Lucre
massacre	Massacre
mediocre	Mediocre

4.6.2. The Continuous Tense of Verbs Ending with "e"

In American English, the final "e" is removed from verbs before adding "-ing", in correct British English this is not done. However, the American practice of dropping the "e" is becoming quite common in British English.

Examples:

Verb (infinite)	Continuous tense	
	American English	**British English**
To route	routing	routeing
To rhyme	Rhyming	rhymeing

4.6.3. The Continuous, Past Tenses, or Nouns of Verbs Ending with "l"

If a verb ends in a single "l", then the American "-ing", "-ed" and "-er" forms also have a single "l", whereas the British forms have a double "l".

Examples 1:

	American	British
Verb (infinitive)	to signal	to signal
Present Continuous	Signalling	signalling
Past	Signalled	signalled
Noun	Signaller	signaller

Examples 2:

	American English	British English
Verb (infinitive)	to model	to model
Present Continuous	modeling	modelling
Past	modeled	modelled
Noun	modeler	modeller

4.6.4. The "-ize" vs. "-ise"; Likewise the "-Ization" vs. "–Isation" (The "-*yse*" vs "-*yze*")

American English uses -ize ending for verbs and their derived nous "-ization", whereas British English uses "-ise" and "–isation" in most cases. American spelling accepts only "-ize" endings in most cases, such as organize, recognize, and realize. However, the British usage sometimes (and rarely) accepts "–ize". Similarly, the British use "–yse", while the American usage is "–yze"

Example 1: The verbs

American	British
civilize	civilise
characterize	characterise
organize	organise
patronize	patronise
recognize	recognise

Example 2: The nouns

American	British
patronization	patronisation
organization	organisation
civilization	civilisation
characterization	characterisation

Example 3: The "-yse" vs "–yze"

American	British
analyze	analyse
catalyze	catalyse
hydrolyze	hydrolyse
paralyze	paralyse

However, some verbs ending in -*ize* or -*ise* are not interchangeable, depending on the variety usage – some verbs take the –*ze* form exclusively, whereas others take only –*se*.

Examples:

		The words
a.	Exclusively –*ze*	*capsize, seize*
b.	Exclusively –*se*	advertise, advise, arise, incise, excise, comprise, compromise, demise, despise, devise, disguise, exercise, improvise, merchandise, revise, supervise, surprise, and televise

4.6.5. The "-*ce*" vs the "-*se*"

In most cases nouns ending in -*ce* are derived from verbs ending in -*se* verb forms. Both American English and British English retain the noun/verb distinction, but American English has abandoned the distinction where the two words in each pair are homophones, while British spelling retains. American English uses practice and license for both meanings. In addition, American English spelling ending with –*se* are used for nouns derived from verbs ending in –*nd*.

Example 1: Where the distinction is retained

	American		British	
	Verb	**Noun**	**Verb**	**Noun**
a	advise	advice	advise	advice
b.	devise	device	devise	device

Example 2: Where the distinction has been abandoned in American usage

	American		British	
	Verb	**Noun**	**Verb**	**Noun**
a.	licence	licence	license	licence
b.	practise	practise	practise	practice

Example 3: General preference for -*se*

	American		British	
	Verb	Noun	Verb	Noun
a.	defend	defense	defend	licence
b.	offend	offense	offend	practice
c.	pretend	pretense	pretend	pretence

4.6.6. The "-*xion*" vs the "-*ction*"

The spellings of nouns ending in"-*xion*" are now used under rare special circumstances in everyday British usage, while they are not used at all in the American usage:

Examples:

American	British	
	Common	Rear usage
connection	connection	connexion
Inflection	Inflection	inflexion
deflection	deflection	deflexion
Reflection	reflection	reflexion

4.6.6. The "-*ogue*" vs the "-*og*"

Some words end either in -*ogue* or in –*og*. The -*ogue* endings are the standard in British usage, while in American usage, –og is preferred.

Example:

American	British
analog	analogue
catalog	catalogue
dialog	dialogue
demagog	demagogue

4.6.7. Simplification of *ae* (*æ*) and *oe* (*œ*)

Many words written with *ae/æ* or *oe/œ* in British English are written with a single *e* in American English.

Examples:

American	British
anemia	anaemia
anesthesia	anaesthesia
cesium	caesium
diarrhea	diarrhoea
hemophilia	haemophilia
leukemia	leukaemia
estrogen	oestrogen

4.6.8. Compounds and Hyphens

British English often prefers hyphenated compounds, whereas American English discourages the use of hyphens in compounds. Where there is no compelling reason, the use of single-word form is much more common in American usage.

Examples:

American	British
Editor in chief	Editor-in-chief
counterattack	counter-attack
forever	for ever
anymore	any more
nearby	near by

4.6.9. Acronyms and Abbreviations

Contractions, where the final letter is present, are often written in British English without full stops, while the final letter is not present, generally do take full stops. In American English, abbreviations always require a full stop.

Examples:

	American	British
With final letter	Mr.	Mr
	Mrs.	Mrs
	Dr.	Dr
	St.	St
Without final letter	vol.	vol.
	etc.	etc.
	ed.	ed.

4.6.10. Use of the Present Perfect

In British English, the present perfect is used to express an action that has occurred in the recent past that has an effect on the present moment.

Example:

	Statement
American	I lost my key. Can you help me look for it?
British	I have lost my key. Can you help me look for it?

However, both forms are generally accepted in standard American English. Other differences involving the use of the present perfect in British English and simple past in American English include already, just, and yet.

Example:

	Statement
American	(a) I just had lunch.
	or
	I have just had lunch.
	(b) I have already seen that film.
	Alternatively
	I already saw that film.
	(c) Have you finished your homework yet?
	Alternatively
	Did you finish your homework yet?
British	(a) I have just had lunch.
	(b) I have already seen that film.

(c) Have you finished your homework yet?

4.6.11. Possession

There are two forms to express possession in English, "have" or "have got".

Example:

	American	British
Question	Do you have a laser microscope?	Have you got a laser microscope?
Answer	We do not have a laser microscope.	We have (got) no laser microscope.

4.6.12. Use of some Verbs

The differences in using some verb forms like "get"

For example:

American	Nayel has gotten much better at playing squash.
British	Nayel has got much better at playing squash.

4.6.13. Vocabulary

Probably, the major differences between British and American English rests in the choice of vocabulary. Some words mean different things in the two varieties.

Examples 1: Same word different meaning

Word	American	British
Mean	angry	not generous
	bad humoured	tight fisted
Anaesthetist (Anesthetist)	nurse or technician trained to administer anaesthesia	physician trained to administer anaesthesia
Mad	angry	mental sickness (state of craziness)

To appropriate	to dispense (money), to budget	to take something (e.g. money) to oneself
Athlete	one who participates in sports in general	one who participates in running, throwing, and jumping competitions

Examples 2: Same meaning different words or expression

	American	British
Profession of financial calculation	Accounting	Accountancy[8]
Direction opposite to clockwise	counterclockwise	anti-clockwise
Medical profession inadminister anesthesia	anaesthesiologist	anaesthetist
Chemist	Pharmacist Pharmacy	druggist drugstore

4.6.14. Prepositions

There are also a few differences in preposition use including the following:

	American English	British English
a.	on the weekend	at the weekend
b.	in a team	on a team
c.	Please write to me soon	Please write me soon
d.	Meet with the professor tomorrow	Meet the professor tomorrow

4.6.15. Past Simple/Past Participles

A few verbs have two or more acceptable forms of the past simple or past participle in both American and British English, however, the irregular form is generally more common in British English and the regular form is more common in American English.

---

[8] In United Kingdom, accounting is the school subject, while accountancy is the professional qualification.

Examples:

Verb	Past simple or Past participles	
	American English	**British English**
burn	burned	burnt
dream	dreamed	dreamt
lean	leaned	leant
learn	learned	learnt
smell	smelled	smelt
spell	spelled	spelt
spill	spilled	spilt
spoil	spoiled	spoilt

For a more complete list of the vocabulary differences between British and American English, see the appendix and visit a few websites that detail the differences (e.g. Mr Peter Burden's Home page on http://www.scit. wlv.ac.uk/~jphb/american.html).

4.7. CLEARING FOG OF ARTICLES

Most English as a First Language (EFL) writers rarely give articles (*a, an,* and *the*) a second thought. However, for writers of English as a Second Language (ELS), they can be the tricky. Particularly for German writers, appropriate use of articles are a major problem because German has many forms of articles and they do not follow the same principles as English. Consequently, there is a tendency of over using articles by most German ESL. For other English as a Second Language writers, articles are frequently omitted, probably because some languages do not have articles. Many scientific writers tend to omit the articles for sake of brevity or to save space [61]. However, consistent omission of the articles can hamper comprehension of the scientific and technical material, therefore, selections of the right article for the right situation are very important in scientific writing as it is in general English speaking. English has only two types of articles: indefinite (*a,* or *an*); and definite (*the*).

4.7.1. Indefinite Articles *a* and *an*

A and *an* signal that the noun modified is indefinite, referring to any member of a group. These indefinite articles are used with singular nouns when the noun is general; the corresponding indefinite quantity word *some* is used for plural general nouns.

The rules of application are:
(i) *a* should be used in combination with singular nouns beginning with a consonant, while *an* should be used in combination with singular nouns beginning with a vowel.
Example:
A   metal, scientist, chemist, etc
An artist, environment, equipment, etc.
(ii) If the noun is modified by an adjective, the choice between *a* and *an* depends on the initial sound of the adjective that immediately follows the article.
Examples:
(a) A broken egg
(b) An unusual problem
(iii) *a* should be used if the noun begins with a vowel but has a consonant sound.
Examples:
(a) a user (sounds like 'yoo-zer,' i.e. begins with a consonant 'y' sound, so 'a' is used)
(b) a uranium atom (sounds like 'yoo-ranium,' i.e. begins with consonant 'y' sound)
(iv) *a* should also be used when using a proper noun to indicate characteristics of the named person
Example:
(a) He is a master in project funding negotiations.
(v) *a* should also be used to mean "a certain person whose name is"
Example:
(a) A Dr. Tyhoda called this morning.
(vi) Indefinite articles are also used to indicate membership in a profession, nation, or religion.
Examples:
(a) Msau is a biologist.
(b) Martin is a Malawian.

(c) Udaya Gurungu is a practicing Buddhist.
(vii) *Some* should be used in combination with indefinite plural nouns.
Example:
(a) Some scientists
(b) Some uranium

4.7.2. Definite Article "*the*"

The definite article is used before singular and plural nouns when the noun is particular or specific. The signals that the noun is definite, that it refers to a particular member of a group. However, there are some rules on condition to use *the* or not. Rules on where "the" should be used:

§	Rules
1	The article "the" should be used for surnames in the plural. For example, Wrong Keydels will fly with us to Malawi. Right The Keydels will fly with us to Malawi.

2	The article "the" should always be used with uncountable nouns that are made more specific by a limiting modifying phrase or clause.
	Examples
	a. Wrong Water is too acidic to drink.
	     Right The water is too acidic to drink.
	b. Wrong Reviewer, who recommended the article to be rejected, was inexperienced.
	     Right The reviewer, who recommended the article to be rejected, was inexperienced.
	c. Wrong Toxicity of uranium to *Lemna gibba* is variable but undeniable.
	     Right The toxicity of uranium to *Lemna gibba* is variable but undeniable.

3	The article "the" should always be used when a noun refers to something unique. Examples: i. The proteomic laboratory ii. The theory of relativity iii The research budget

4	The article "the" should be used for nouns identified by a special adjective. Examples:

	Superlative	i.	The most important consequence
		ii.	The highest concentration
	Particular (ordinal)	i.	The second phase
	number	ii.	The twentieth anniversary

5	The article "the" should be used in combination with nouns referring to a thing, issue, or event previously mentioned. Example: i. The problems you identified in today's meeting is very important. ii. The method you are using is outdated

6	"The" should be used in reference to a time or place treated as one collective unit. For example,

	Time	i.	the teens
		ii.	the sixties
	Place	i.	the sun
		ii.	the earth

7	"The" should be used in reference to knowledge the writer or speaker and audience share. Example: i. the recent field test in Lengefeld ii. the wetland project

8	"The" should be used in reference to a particular object or research equipment. For example:

	Wrong	Switch on UV-vis-Spectrophotometer as recommended.
	Right	Switch on the UV-vis-Spectrophotometer as recommended.

9.	"The" is used to distinguish between people, things, or even instruments with the same name. For example: i. Jochen Foerster, who sold me the computer, is not the multi-talented Jochen Foerster. ii. The nanoplotter used in the experiment is not the modern nanoplotter.

10	"The" should be used with most acronyms that have separately pronounced letters, but no article should be used with an acronym that

can be pronounces as a word.

Example:

| With article | The U.N., The U.S.A., The BMBF, The DGL, The BMU, The DGF. |
| Without article | NATO, DAAD, SETAC, DECHEMA, UNEP, etc. |

| 11 | "The" is used when the article is part of an accepted proper name, such as a ship, journal, desert, group, hotel, etc. |

Examples:

Wrong	hotel	The Hilton
	magazine	The Nature Magazine
	ship	The Titanic
	desert	The Sahara
	group	The Beatles
	organization	The United Nations
Correct	hotel	The Hilton
	Magazine	The Nature Magazine
	ship	The Titanic
	Desert	The Sahara
	Group	The Beatles
	Organization	The United Nations

4.7.3. Rules in the Use of "*the*" with Geographical Features

The rules for using the article "the" with geographical features are as follows:

§	Rule
1	Do not use *the* before names of physical sites like continents, countries or states (except countries or kingdoms composed of a number of states), cities and towns, likewise, street name.

Examples:

	Wrong	Correct
Continents	The Africa	Africa
	The Europe	Europe
	The Asia	Asia
Countries	The Germany	Germany
	The Malawi	Malawi

	Wrong	Correct
	The Zambia	Zambia
Countries or kingdoms composed of several states	Netherlands	The Netherlands
	USA	The USA
	United Kingdom (UK)	The United Kingdom (The UK)
Cities or towns	The Dresden	Dresden
	The Leipzig	Leipzig
	The Lilongwe	Lilongwe
	The Blantyre	Blantyre
Streets	The Hochschul Street	Hochschul Street
	The Hallwachs Street	Hallwachs Street
	The Victoria Avenue	Victoria Avenue
	The Kamuzu Highway	Kamuzu Highway

2   Do not use *the* before names of physical features like mountains, oceans, lakes, and rivers, as well as islands, except where they are a group or ranges of mountains

Examples:

	Wrong	**Correct**
Mountains	The Mount Everest	Mount Everest
	The Mount Mulanje	Mount Mulanje
Ranges	Alps	The Alpes
	Andes	The Andes
Lakes	The Lake Malawi	Lake Malawi
	The Lake Victoria	Lake Victoria
	Great Lakes	the Great Lakes
Islands	The Rügen Island	Rügen Island
	The Likoma Island	Likoma Island
	Zanzibar	The Zanzibar
	Canary Islands	The Canary Islands

3   "The" is used before names of physical features like rivers, oceans, and seas with accepted proper name, points on the globe, and geographical areas.

Examples:

		Wrong	Correct
a.	Features with accepted proper name	Nile	The Nile
		Indian Ocean	The Indian ocean

		Pacific	The Pacific
b.	Points on the globe	Equator	The Equator
		North Pole	The North Pole
c.	Geographical areas	Middle East	The Middle East
		West	The West
		Sub-Sahara	The Sub-Sahara

4.7.4. Where Articles Are not Required

Generally, no articles should be used before uncountable nouns referring to something in a general sense. For instance, no article is required before nouns that refer to physical masses without distinct form or shape, an abstract concept, ongoing processes, and a field of study or endeavour.

Examples:

Noun description	Wrong	Right
Physical masses without	The water	water
distinct form or shape	The sand	sand
	The acid	acid
Abstract concept	The gravity	gravity
	The information	information
	The justice	justice
	The satisfaction	satisfaction
	The racism	racism
	The dictatorship	Dictatorship
Ongoing processes	The respiration	respiration
	The growth	growth
	The pollution	pollution
	The communication	communication
Field of study or endeavour	The engineering	engineering
	The nanotechnology	nanotechnology
	The photonics	photonics
	The materials science	materials science
	The squash	squash
	The karat	karat

Further, no article should be used with common nouns used as terms of address and usually capitalised.

Example:

Wrong	**The** Professor Dudel is chairing the Ph.D. examination commission
Correct	Professor Dudel is chairing the Ph.D. examination commission

4.8. CLEARING THE FOG OF PUNCTUATIONS

Punctuations are placed in text to make meaning clear and to make reading easier [62]. The various punctuation marks perform the following four functions:

	Function
1	They separate (a period separates sentences)
2	They group or enclose (parentheses enclose extraneous information)
3	They connect (a hyphen connects a unit modifier)
4	They impart meaning (a question mark may make an otherwise declarative sentence interrogative)

The function of a punctuation mark is the basis for the rules governing its use and should be the basis for determining whether it is needed or not. The modern tendency is to punctuate to prevent misreading (open style) rather than to use all punctuation that the grammatical structure will allow (close style). Although the open style results in a more inviting product, it does allow subjectivity, perhaps arbitrariness, in the use of some marks, for example, the comma and hyphen.

Consistency in the author or editor's subjective decisions is vital to a well-punctuated report. This chapter addresses the marks of punctuation, in alphabetical order, presenting their functions, situations when the marks are required or incorrect, and situations when the marks are appropriate but optional. Because the exclamation point is so rare in technical writing, it is not covered herein. Guidelines for its use parallel those for the question mark.

4.8.1. Apostrophe

The apostrophe (') may be the simplest and yet most frequently misused mark of punctuation in English, as well as in scientific writing. Here are the guidelines for using the mark correctly.

§	Guiding rules

1   An apostrophe may be used to indicate possession.

    i.   Use an apostrophe plus -s to show the possessive form of a singular noun, even if that singular noun already ends in –s

        Examples:

        a.   Martin's book

        b.   biologist's tool

    ii.   To form the possessive of a plural noun that already ends in -s, add only an apostrophe without -s

        Examples:

        a.   Jones' book

        b.   Biologists' assembly

2   An apostrophe is never used to form the possessive of a personal pronoun. However, an apostrophe plus -s should be added to form the possessive of some indefinite pronouns:

    Examples:

    Personal   hers, his, its, ours, yours, theirs

    Indefinite   a.   somebody's work

              b.   one's personal responsibility

              c.   anybody's guess

3   An apostrophe should not be used to form the plurals of nouns including dates, acronyms, and family names. As a general rule, use only an **-s** (or an **-es**) without an apostrophe to form the plurals.

    Examples:

Acronyms	Wrong	The data is backed up on CD's.
	Correct	The data is backed up on CDs.
Time	Wrong	The uranium prospecting was studied in the 1990's.
	Correct	The uranium prospecting was studies in the 1990s.

4   To form the plural of a word or a letter referred to as the word or letter itself, but the apostrophe is not necessary when the word retains its meaning.

    Example:

    a.   meaning no conditions   there can be no ands, ifs, and buts

    b.   meaning the word itself   there can be no and's, if's, and but's

5   To indicate omitted characters in contractions, be careful to place the apostrophe where the letter or letters have been omitted, which is not always

the same place where the two words have been joined.
Examples:

Word or phrase	Contraction
a. Government	Gov't
b. National	nat'l

6 An apostrophe plus –s should be use and added to the last noun listed when two or more nouns possess the same thing. However, when two or more nouns separately possess something, an apostrophe should be added to each noun listed.
Examples:

Possessing the same thing	a.	Bettina and Klaus's alginate capsules
	b.	Nanoplotter and contact printer's computer
Separately possess something	a.	Nanokat's and biorat's project milestones
	b.	Katharina's and Jan's offices

4.8.2. Brackets

Brackets are considered an insertion mark. The nonmathematical function of brackets is to inform readers that the author is making a comment, criticising, explaining further, showing omission, clarifying, injecting, or giving more information, and in reference citations. Brackets are considered quieter than parentheses. Parentheses are used to clarify meaning or to insert supplemental information in all types of writing. Brackets are used mainly for clarification within quoted material. However, the term 'brackets' is commonly used in scientific writing to describe both square brackets [these] and round brackets (these) which include function of parenthesis. The rules of thumb in the use of brackets in scientific writing are as explained below:

§	Rule
1	Insert brackets in sentences before and after editorial comments. It clarifies the information for the reader.
2	Use brackets when inserting material into sentences that are not originally in the sentence – in other words, not done by the original author.
3	Add brackets in sentences to clarify information that is already in parentheses.
4	Use brackets when starting a sentence with a quote that is not capitalized.

Any deviation in a quote should be shown in brackets.

5   Use brackets where Latin abbreviations like e.g., and i.e., are used.
     Examples:
     i.   Some metals (e.g. iron) co-precipitate with arsenic in surface water.
     ii.   Bioreduction of uranium occurs when an electron donor are present
           (i.e. an organic substance that will release and electron use to transfer
           energy in the bacteria).

6   Use brackets to show incorrect spelling. Usually, the Latin term "sic",
     which means "thus", should be used to alert the reader that the word may
     be misspelled in the original document. Brackets are used around the
     word like [sic] (*also see rule §9*).

7   Put brackets around nonessential information. Brackets are used when
     authors wish to say something that is not important at all.

8   Spaces should not be used after the left bracket or before the right bracket.

9   Use round brackets to indicate an aside, an associated remark, or an
     additional piece of information, which is closely related to the main
     subject of the sentence in which it is placed.
     Example:
     i.   The professor argues that Evolon Model (of which he does really
           understand) would not predict the uranium ecotoxicity effectively
           because of hermetic responses.

10   Use square brackets "[x]" to indicate that something has been added to the
     original text for purposes of clarification or comment by someone editing.
     Example:
     i.   The speciation simulation predicts that this species [uranyl
           diphosphate] hardly occurs in surface mine water.
     ii.   A student wrote that arsenic 'does not oxydise [sic] easily from 3rd to
           5th oxidation as previously known'.

11   When brackets are used at the end of a sentence, the full stop falls outside
     the bracket.
     Example:
     i.   Our son Chizi should work hard (as this one does).

12   Any statement within brackets should be grammatically independent of the
     sentence in which it occurs. That is, the sentence should be complete,
     even if the contents of the brackets were to be removed.
     Example:
     i.   The American professor (who was visiting Dresden as external
           examiner in my DSc commission) had also several invited talks and
           lectures.

| 13 | Keep the expressions within brackets as brief as possible, to avoid interrupting the flow of the sentence in which they are placed. |
| 14 | The use of brackets should be kept to a minimum. If used too frequently, they create a fog in the writing – an unsettling effect. |

4.8.3. Colon

The function of the colon is to introduce or separate lists, clauses, and quotations, along with several conventional uses. Actually, it is an elegant way of introducing a list, and at the same time, emphasizing the elements of the list by separating them from the rest of the sentence. Such lists might consist of words, prepositional phrases, infinitive, noun, or even clauses. A colon has the same separating force as a full stop that it brings a sentence almost to a stop. Rule thumb for correct use of introductory colons are:

§	Rule
1	No colon must be used between a verb or preposition and its direct object. Examples: a. Wrong — The techniques of extracting uranium from its ore deposits are: open-pit, underground, *in-situ* leaching, and borehole mining. Correct — The techniques of extracting uranium from its ore deposits are open-pit, underground, *in-situ* leaching, and borehole mining. b. Wrong — The *in-situ* mining procedure composed **of**: boreholes drilling, injection of water at high pressure through, break-up of the ore-bearing rocks, pumping the slurry, and the dewatering to recover the uranium. *Correct* — The *in-situ* mining procedure composed of boreholes drilling, injection of water at high pressure through, break-up of the ore-bearing rocks, pumping the slurry, and the dewatering to recover the uranium.
2	No colon should be used after introductory phases as such , that is, for example, and such as. Example: Wrong — PhreeqC is used for simulation of geochemical parameters such as: chemical speciation, sorption dynamic, and one

dimension transport dynamic.

Correct   PhreeqC is used for simulation of geochemical parameters such as chemical speciation, sorption dynamic, and one dimension transport dynamic.

3   When items of a list are numbered, the numbers do not affect the punctuation. However, colon should never be used merely to emphasizes the material that follows, where separation is not grammatically desirable.

Examples:

Wrong   The predicted arsenic species from PhreeqC modeling are: (1) NaH_2AsO_4, (2) $Na_2HAsO_4^-$, and (3) AsO_4^{3-}.

Correct   The predicted arsenic species from PhreeqC modeling are (1) NaH_2AsO_4, (2) $Na_2HAsO_4^-$, and (3) AsO_4^{3-}.

4   A colon should be used to introduce a list in opposition to a noun.

Example:

Wrong   Uranium occurs mainly in three isotopes a ^{238}U, a ^{235}U, and ^{234}U.

Correct   Uranium occurs mainly in three isotopes: a ^{238}U, a ^{235}U, and ^{234}U.

5   A colon should be used to introduce a list whose introductory statement contains the words as follows or the following.

Examples:

Wrong   The research group consists of the following the bionanotechnology subgroup, the nanobiotechnology subgroup, and the environmental engineering.

Correct   The research group consists of the following: the bionanotechnology subgroup, the nanobiotechnology subgroup, and the environmental engineering.

6   A colon should be used to introduce a list that amplifies an introductory sentence.

Examples:

Wrong   The purpose of this report is twofold to evaluate the performance of the instruments and to expand the database.

Correct   The purpose of this report is twofold: to evaluate the performance of the instruments and to expand the database.

7   A colony should be used with numbering to emphasize a list, and at the same time, make a long list easy to read.

Example:

The research group consists of the following:

the bionanotechnology subgroup;
the nanobiotechnology subgroup; and,
the environmental engineering.

8   No colon should be used when the introduction to a displayed list is not a complete sentence.
Example:
The purposes of this report are
1. To evaluate the performance of the instruments
2. To expand the data base

9   A colon may be used between two clauses when the second amplifies or restates the first.
Example:

| Wrong | The physiological regulation processes resulting from ion homeostasis at the particular ion stoichiometry imbalance, directly influence the internalisation dynamics of the metal, if these transport pathways are implicated in its uptake. |
| Correct | The physiological regulation processes resulting from ion homeostasis: at the particular ion stoichiometry imbalance, directly influence the internalisation dynamics of the metal, if these transport pathways are implicated in its uptake. |

10   Colon may be used conventionally
Examples:
a.   Between hours and minutes in time: 11:30 a.m.
b.   To express ratios: 2:1 mixture.

4.8.4. Comma

The primary functions of the comma are to separate and to enclose elements of a sentence. Of all the marks of punctuation, the comma requires the most judgment because punctuating with commas does not only require compliance with a set of rules, but also the understanding of the material being punctuated. If poorly punctuated, commas can change the entire meaning of the statement[9]. As a result, the advice on how best to punctuate with commas will be divided into (a) commas that separate, and (b) commas that enclose.

---

[9] A major source of fog in a number of manuscripts, which I have peer reviewed, are due to omission or misplacement of comma.

(i) Separating Commas

Many separating uses of the comma are optional in an open style. When commas are used without careful consideration, they chop up the text and can even render it difficult to read, contrary to the purpose of punctuation. Thus, the rules of thumb to punctuate with a comma of this case are as follows:

§	Rule of the thumb
1	A comma may separate independent clauses joined by coordinate conjunctions.

Example:

Inappropriate	The artifacts dominate the spectrum but the fluorescence peaks are distinctively high.
Appropriate	The artifacts dominate the spectrum, but the fluorescence peaks are distinctively high.

2	When the independent clauses are short and closely related, the comma may be omitted.

Example:

Inappropriate	Each performance of an experiment is called a trial, and its result is called an outcome.
Appropriate	Each performance of an experiment is called a trial and its result is called an outcome.

3	The comma is usually retained between clauses joined by the coordinate conjunctions but and for, purely to emphasize the contrast. In such a case the following sub-rules apply:

a)   When the independent clause is complicated and contains internal commas, a semicolon should be used to separate them instead of a comma.

Inappropriate	The arsenic distributions in the sediment partitions were similar in wetland ponds without vegetation but larger differences occurred in vegetated ponds.
Appropriate	The arsenic distributions in the sediment partitions were similar in wetland ponds without vegetation, but larger differences occurred in vegetated ponds.

b)   Do not use a comma to separate independent clauses without a coordinate conjunction

Example:

Inappropriate	The arsenic distributions in the sediment

| | partitions were similar in wetland ponds without vegetation, however, larger differences occurred in vegetated ponds. |
| Appropriate | The arsenic distributions in the sediment partitions were similar in wetland ponds without vegetation; however, larger differences occurred in vegetated ponds. |

4   Do not separate compound predicates with a comma unless they are long and require a comma for clarity.

Example:

| Wrong | Addition of phosphates reduces the biouptake of arsenic, and decreases the apparent toxicity of arsenic to the bacteria. |
| Correct | Addition of phosphates reduces the biouptake of arsenic and decreases the apparent toxicity of arsenic to the bacteria. |

5   A comma may not sufficiently separate compound and long predicates. The best is to construct several sentences.

Example:

| Inappropriate | Metal content was determined with ICP-MS, chemical speciation was simulated with PhreeqC codes, and total phosphorus was measured with UV-Vis Spectrophotometer. |
| Appropriate | Metal content was determined with ICP-MS. Chemical speciation was simulated with PhreeqC codes. Total phosphorus was measured with UV-Vis Spectrophotometer. |

6   A comma is required to separate a series of three or more elements.

Examples:

| Wrong | The PhreeqC geochemical modeling codes can also predict chemical species of the media, and mineral phase development. |
| Correct | The PhreeqC geochemical modeling codes can also predict chemical species of the media, sorption kinetics, two-dimension transport, saturation indices, and mineral phase development. |

7   A comma may be used to separate an introductory phrase or clause from the main clause.

Examples:

a.   If the variable t is actually time, then μ is specific growth rate.

b.   As revealed in Figure 1, the biodegradation of MTBE is dependent on source of carbon and media flow rate.

8   A comma should always be put after all introductory clauses and all introductory phrases containing a verb form.

Example:

a.   Although some scientists do not agree with the definition of bioefficiency, it is currently appearing often in literature.

b.   In conducting sequential extraction, we try to determine the main sink of arsenic in the sediment.

9   A comma is optional after a short introductory adverbial phrase unless the comma is required for clarity.

Example:

1st option   Soon after the photon density becomes steady as gains and losses balance each other.

2nd option   Soon after, the photon density becomes steady as gains and losses balance each other.

10   A comma should not be placed after an introductory phrase that immediately precedes the verb it modifies

Example:

Wrong   Only in recent years, has the mechanism of arsenic biomineralisation been explained.

Correct   Only in recent years has the mechanism of arsenic biomineralisation been explained.

11   A comma is appropriate after an internal phrase or clause, but it is not appropriate before the phrase or clause unless it is non-restrictive. A comma should follow, but does not precede a restrictive introductory elements.

Example:

Wrong   Diffusion flux is faster than sorption on biological interface, and, after equilibrium is reached on the biological interface, both are slower than internalisation flux.

Correct   Diffusion flux is faster than sorption on the biological interface, and after equilibrium is achieved, both are slower than the internalisation flux.

12   A comma should precede and follow non-restrictive introductory elements.

Examples:

Wrong   Note that even though the metals are dissolved and free ions, the macrophytes take up only bioavailable species.

Correct   Note that, even though the metals are dissolved and free ions, the macrophytes take up only bioavailable species.

13 A comma should separate only consecutive adjectives that are coordinate[10]. Deciding whether an adjective is coordinate or not can be tricky; when in doubt, do not insert the comma between the adjectives because the comma only adds emphasis to the adjectives.

14 A comma should be used to indicate the omission element when clauses in a sentence contain repeated elements (e.g., verb)
    Example:

Wrong	Uranium content was determined with ICP-MS; arsenic with AAS and total phosphorus with UV-Vis Spectrophotometer.
Correct	Metal content was determined with ICP-MS; arsenic, with AAS, and total phosphorus, with UV-Vis Spectrophotometer.

15 The comma may be omitted when the clauses are short
    Example:

1st Option	Uranium content was determined with ICP-MS and total phosphorus, with UV-Vis Spectrophotometer.
2nd Option	Uranium content was determined with ICP-MS, and total phosphorus with UV-Vis Spectrophotometer.

16 A comma should be used to separate a direct quotations and questions from the rest of the sentence.
    Example:

Wrong	In section 2, the authors state "Bioreduction of uranium occurs under anaerobic and low calcium condition".
Correct	In section 2, the authors' state, "Bioreduction of uranium occurs under anaerobic and low calcium condition".

17 Never use a comma to set off an indirect quotation or one that is part of the grammatical structure of the sentence.
    Example:

Wrong	In section 2, the authors' state, that bioreduction of uranium occurs under anaerobic and low calcium condition.
Correct	In section 2, the authors state that bioreduction of uranium occurs under anaerobic and low calcium condition.

---

[10] Adjectives are coordinate if (1) they can be linked by "and" and (2) they independently modify the noun.

(ii) Enclosing Commas

An enclosing comma is used to set off words, phrases, or clauses that break into the normal word order of a sentence. The enclosed material may be removed without changing the grammatical structure of the sentence. The enclosing comma requires a partner, which may be another comma or a colon, semicolon, period, question mark, or exclamation mark. The rule guiding the used of commas that enclose are as follows:

§	Rule of the thumb
1	Commas must enclose non-restrictive modifiers.

Examples:

Wrong (a) The results may not be continuous but may, in fact, be digital data.

(b) The second integral, being the integral of an odd function over even limits, is zero.

Correct (a) The results may not be continuous but may, in fact, be digital data.

(b) The second integral, being the integral of an odd function over even limits, is zero.

Remark The non-restrictive prepositional and verbal phrases are enclosed with commas

2 Non-restrictive relative clauses should be enclosed with commas.

Example:

Restrictive The most dependable is the thermodynamic database, which researchers at Dresden-Rossendorf developed to include most of the organic compounds.

Non-restrictive The most dependable is the thermodynamic database of researchers at Dresden-Rossendorf, which was developed to include most of the organic compounds.

3 A comma should enclose non-restrictive adverbial clauses.

Example:

Restrictive The last chapter introduces highlights areas where research is in progress.

Non-restrictive The relationship between internal and external metal is presented in figure 2, where arrows represent a shift in bioefficiency.

4 (a) Whether restrictive or non-restrictive, a comma should separate an

introductory adverbial clause from the clause it modifies.

(b) When an internal adverbial clause precedes the clause that it modifies, a comma is not necessary before the clause unless it is clearly non-restrictive

Example:

Wrong   Biosorption rate is larger than internalisation rate, and, after equilibrium is achieved, both are smaller than diffusion flux rate to biological interface.

Correct   Biosorption rate is larger than internalisation rate and, after equilibrium is achieved, both are smaller than diffusion flux rate to biological interface.

5   Commas should enclose words or phrases in apposition unless the appositive is restrictive. A restrictive appositive is required to distinguish its antecedent from other members of the same class.

Example:

Restrictive   The noble gas argon is used as the ion-carrier gas into ICP-MS chamber.

Non-restrictive   Argon, the lightest noble gas that does not get ionised easily, is used as ion-carrier gas into ICP-MS chamber.

Remark:

When dashes enclose appositives, particularly when the appositive already contains commas, they improve clarity.

6   Commas should be omitted around symbolic appositives regardless of being restrictive or not.

Example:

Restrictive   The coefficients B_{eff}, and B_{ads} are plotted in figure 1.

Non-restrictive   The biological coefficient B_{eff} is plotted in figure 1.

7   It is optional and preferential to enclose non-restrictive symbolic appositives with commas.

Example:

Non-restrictive   The uptake parameters are in the model, and are compared with measured values in Table 1.

8   Commas may optionally enclosed non-restrictive parenthetical phrases, rhetorical adverbs, antithetical phrases, introductory words, and other interruptive sentence elements.

Example:

Parenthetical phrase   Chemical speciation data used herein, such as arsenic speciation, have been

	computed with PhreeqC with a self-developed thermodynamic database.
Rhetorical adverb	The redox status of mine water cannot be estimated precisionally; it can be assumed, however, to lie between -20 and 450 mV.
Antithetical elements	In aquatic systems, the oxidation of As III to As V is not spontaneous, not the electron from uranium as most geochemist are accustomed to believing.
Interruptive words or phrases	For most nanoparticles, for example, breach of fluorescence occurs in very small ones.

9   Commas should enclose a phrase with termination that also reads back to a previous phrase.
    Example:

Incorrect	Uranium ion interacting with phosphate will form complexes if not all precipitate.
Correct	Uranium ion interacting with phosphate will form complexes, if not all, precipitate.

10   A comma should enclose, as a nominative absolute phrase (i.e., a noun with no grammatical function in the sentence modified by a participle) because a nominative absolute phrase is non-restrictive.
    Example:

Incorrect	Most dependables may be arsenic data from freeze-dried plant samples more values obtained from freeze-dried sample having a low standard deviation.
Correct	Most dependables may be arsenic data from freeze-dried plant samples, more values obtained from freeze-dried sample having a low standard deviation.

4.8.5. Dash

Like the comma, a dash "–" is used both to enclose and to separate. A dash suggests a definite tone, often a note of surprise or an emphasis equivalent to a mild exclamation. However, a dash looses all its distinctiveness and becomes a sloppy substitute for conventional punctuation when used regularly in place of commas, colons, or semicolons. Rules that govern correct use of dashes can also be separated into enclosing and separating dashes, just like what we did for the comma (above).

(i) Enclosing Dashes[11]

An enclosing dash is a replacement for an enclosing comma in order to add emphasis. Dashes may replace commas in enclosing interrupting elements and non-restrictive modifiers and appositives. Here are the guiding rules:

§	Rule of the thumb
1	Dashes are appropriate when a comma is misleading (especially serial commas)
	Example:
	Confusing The lasant gas, argon, and 3He were allowed to mix for 45 minutes.
	Better The lasant gas–argon–and 3He were allowed to mix for 45 minutes.
2	Dashes are also appropriate when the enclosed element contains internal commas.
	Example:
	a. Of the lasant gases studied – argon, xenon, krypton, and neon – argon offers the most promise.
	b. The most promising lasant gas – argon, which is the lightest gas studied – produced a laser output power of 4 W
3	Use dashes when the enclosed element needs emphasis.
	Example:
	Wrong The one-sided spectrum, engineers call it simply "spectrum," is the output of most spectral analyzers.
	Correct The one-sided spectrum – engineers call it simply "spectrum" – is the output of most spectral analyzers.
4	A sentence that is complete and interrupts another should be enclose by dashes

---

[11] Dashes or parentheses are more appropriate when commas are insufficient to enclose an interrupting sentence. The choice to use commas, dashes, or parentheses to enclose a non-restrictive or interrupting element depends on the relation of the element to the rest of the sentence and on the emphasis, a sentence requires.

    a)   Commas are most frequently used to indicate only a slight separation in thought from the rest of the sentence.

    b)   Dashes are used to emphasise the element enclosed and clarify meaning when the element contains internal commas.

    c)   Parentheses are used to indicate that the enclosed element is only loosely connected to the rest of the sentence.

(ii) A Separating Dash[12]

A dash is used to separate sentence elements under the following rules:

§	Rule of the thumb
1	A dash should be used to separates a group of antecedents from their pronoun when the pronoun is the subject of the sentence

Example:

Incorrect	Thorium, radium, radon, and lead, these are the potentially toxic daughter alimented from the decay series of uranium.
Correct	Thorium, radium, radon, and lead – these are the potentially toxic daughter elements from the decay series of uranium.

2   A dash should be used to separate an item from its explanatory statement in a displayed list

Example:

The anaerobic systems for studying arsenic immobilisation mechanism in the sediments require following:

1. Reactor – The column is filled with sediment and bacterial strains and supplied with the arsenic contaminated water.
2. Peristaltic pump – The closed-loop system delivers 0.3 ml min^{-1} of contaminated water.
3. Gaseous propellants – Nitrogen is supplied from tanks at 0.2 mBar for 20 minutes every two days.

3   A dash can be used to separate two clauses when the second amplifies or restates the first. (The colon or semicolon may also be used for this purpose. The dash is less formal than the colon and more emphatic than the semicolon).

Example:

Incorrect	The tensile strength of the biocer increases with the number of times of soaking in water, where the biocer is dried in an oven before re-soaking
Correct	The tensile strength of the biocer increases with the number of times of soaking in water – where the biocer is dried in an oven before resoaking.

4   A dash may precede a phrase that introduces a summarizing or

---

[12] Use of a comma or semicolon is more appropriate than a dash if an explanatory clause follows the sentence, a semicolon is necessary; if an explanatory phrase follows, a comma is sufficient. If the explanatory phrase or clause receives enough emphasis by being at the end of the sentence, use a comma, or semicolon, whichever appropriate is.

explanatory phrase or clause at the end of a sentence (e.g. that is, namely, and for example), but a comma or semicolon may also be used.

Example:

Inappropriate	The internalization of uranium into Lemna gibba cell depends on the nutrition regime, for example the supply of phosphates, irons and calcium in the medium.
Appropriate	The internalisation of uranium into *Lemna gibba* cell depends on the nutrition regime, for example – the supply of phosphates, irons and calcium in the medium.

(iii) Conventional Uses of Dash

In scientific writing, including environmental sciences, engineering, and technology, a dash may be used by convention. The general accepted conventional uses are as follows:

§	Rules for convention
1	A dash may be used conventionally in scientific writing to separate a title and subtitle.

Example:

Inappropriate	Uranium in water of abandoned uranium mines ecotoxicology and bioremediation implications.
Appropriate	Uranium in water of abandoned uranium mines – ecotoxicology and bioremediation implications.

| 2 | Dash can be used conventionally in vague or open-ended dates. |

Examples:

Formal	The uranium mining has operated from 1994 to an unknown date in the future.
Conventional	The uranium mining has operated from 1994– an unknown date in the future.

4.8.6. Hyphen

The hyphen is used to connect words or parts of words. Mainly, hyphens connect:

(a) the syllables of words broken at the ends of lines;

(b) prefixes and suffixes to words; and,

(c) compound words.

However, the modern trend in scientific writing has moved away from hyphenation.   Nonetheless, the rule of thumb guiding the use of hyphens in scientific writing are grouped below:

(a) End-of-line hyphens

§	The rule of the thumb
1	End-of-line hyphens should be avoided whenever possible. However, where hypanation is extremely necessary, the words may be hyphenated at the ends of lines between syllables.
2	To avoid extremely ragged right margins in unjustified texts, or to avoid large spaces between words in justified text, words may be hyphenated at the ends of lines, only under conditions that: Words are divided only between syllables; No division leaves a single letter at the end or beginning of a line; Two-letter syllables may be left at the end of a line, but two-letter endings may not be carried to the next line; The last word of a paragraph, page, or similar item (e.g., reference citation, figure caption) should not be divided. Hyphenated compounds should be divided only at the hyphen. Solid compounds are divided at the natural breaks (after-body), after prefixes (dis-comfort), and before suffixes (other-wise). Limited consecutive end-of-line hyphens appear in the document.

(b) Hyphen after prefixes and suffixes

§	Rule of the thumb
1	Hyphens are always required with the following prefixes Examples: (a) all- (b) quasihalf- (c) selfquarter- (d) ex-
2	A hyphen should be used to attach a prefix to a proper noun or adjective Example: (a) anti-Globalisation (b) un-Scientific

3   A hyphen is necessary for a homograph (a word with two meanings) that might be misunderstood without the hyphen.

       Examples:

       (a)   coop, co-op
       (b)   multiply, multi-ply
       (c)   unionized, un-ionized
       (d)   recover, re-cover

4   A hyphen is required for a word that might be misread or difficult to read without the hyphen.

       Examples:

       (a)   un-uniform
       (b)   post-stall
       (c)   sub-subcommittee

5   A hyphen is required to avoid a vowel being doubled or a consonant tripled.

       Examples:

       (a)   micro-organism
       (b)   anti-inflation

6   Prefixes co, de, pre, pro, and re should never be hyphenated, even if a vowel will be doubled.

       Examples:

       (a)   cooperation
       (b)   pre-exist
       (c)   reelectrification

7   A hyphen is required to attach a prefix to a hyphenated compound word

       Example:

       (a)   pseudo-steady-state system
       (b)   non-equilibrium-reaction models

8.   A hyphen is necessary to avoid tripling a consonant when attaching a suffix.

       Examples:

       (a)   shell-like
       (b)   hull-less

(c) Hyphenatation of compound words

Compound words are in two forms. The first is where the compound words are permanent in their form, written either solid or hyphenated, and they are determined by usage and often appearing in dictionaries. The second is where the compound words are temporary, which are always hyphenated. Most permanent compounds tend to become solid without hyphen with usage. Here are the rules that guide on identification of compound words that require hyphenation.

§	Rule of the thumb
1	Most permanent prepositional-phrase compound and permanent compound nouns should be hyphenated. Examples: (a) right-of-way (b) mother-in-law

2.	Some noun phrases are in the process of becoming permanent compounds; but although they are defined in the dictionary, they are not yet hyphenated.
	Examples:
	Case 1 used as noun right-of-way
	          used as adjective right-of-way
	Case 2 used as noun state of the art
	          used as adjective state-of-the-art

3.	A hyphen is appropriate when a combination of several nouns are used to form a temporary compound noun as an entity. Examples: (a) staff-writer (b) bench-experiment
4.	A hyphen should be used in an active compound verb derived from a noun form consisting of separate words; however, the passive verb form need not be hyphenated. Examples: Active To cross-check such a function must be integrated. Passive Such a function could be cross checked by integrating.

5.	A unit modifier should not be hyphenated under the following conditions:
	a. When the unit modifier is a predicate adjective.
	      Example:
	      Wrong The biofilter was efficiency tested.
	      Right The biofilter was efficiency-tested.
	b. When the first element of the unit modifier is a comparative or superlative.
	      Example:
	      Wrong higher order calculations
	      Right higher-order calculations

  c. When the first element is an adverb ending with "ly".

    Example:

    Wrong   Relatively accurate prediction

    Right   Relatively accurate-prediction

  d. When the unit modifier is a foreign phrase.

  e. When the unit modifier is a proper name: North Carolina coast (but Anglo-American plan).

  f. When the unit modifier has a letter or number designation as its second element: material 3 properties.

  g. When the unit modifier is enclosed in quotation marks: ``elliptical style" symbol-list.

  h. When the unit modifier is a scientific name of a chemical, an animal, or a plant, which is not normally hyphenated.

    Example:

    Wrong   Nitric-oxide formation

    Right   nitric oxide formation

6. A unit modifier should always be hyphenated under the following conditions:

  a. When the unit modifier contains a past or present participle.

    Example:

    i. speciation-simulated model

    ii. radiation-producing elements

  b. When the unit modifier is a combination of color terms

    Example:

    Wrong   Blue black residue

    Right   blue-black residue

  c. When a connecting word is implied in the unit modifier

    Example:

    i. adsorption-desorption ratio

    ii. Mechaelis-Menten function

  d. When the unit modifier contains numbers (other than number designations).

    Examples:

    Wrong   four degrees of freedom

    Right   four-degrees-of-freedom

4.8.7. Italics[13]

The purpose of italics is to make meaning clear and reading easier. In general writing, they are used to distinguish letters, words, or phrases from the rest of the sentence so that the writer's thought or the meaning and use of the italicised words will be quickly understood. In scientific writing, italics are used to distinguish elements to be emphasized, special terminology, symbols, and words or letters to be differentiated from text. In addition, there are several conventional uses for italics. The following rules of the thumb may be necessary to assist in deciding which words to italicize.

§	The rules of the thumb
1	(a) Italics are especially appropriate for words that would loose the emphasis when written, or for words that will require emphasis when reading the text. Only rarely should a whole sentence be italicized for emphasis, but never a whole passage.
	(b) Overuse of italics to emphasize causes them to loose their force. Therefore, scientific authors should use less and less italics for emphasis by trying to achieve the emphasis by recasting the sentence.
	Examples:
	Italicize for emphasis — Although *the self-cleaning mode* of the nanoplotting was applied, a simple paper test identified the plotting problem.
	Neutral emphasis — The plotting problem was eventually identified not by the self-cleaning mode, but by a simple water test.
2	A key term in a discussion or a technical term accompanied by its definition can be italicised on their first use.
	Example:
	a. The *biofunctionalisation* of ceramic surface for bioremediation is the central focus of the research.
3	Coined terms or technical terms used in a non-standard way, as well as quotes, can be italicized.
	Example:
	a. The *nanoplotted* alginate encapsulate the fluorescent yeast.

---

[13] Italics are usually not listed in most English grammar books as punctuation. Nevertheless, they are considered here for the purpose of effective scientific writing as punctuation.

4	Words used not to represent an idea as usual, but as the words themselves, should be italicized. Likewise, letters used as letters should be italicized. Examples:
	Word Article *an* is used only for words starting with a vowel.
	Letter Press *i* to install the software.
5	Most mathematical symbols and letter symbols representing a physical concept should be italicized, but not chemical symbols, computer symbols, and abbreviations.
6	Foreign words that would be unfamiliar to readers should be italicized, but not foreign proper names, foreign currency, foreign titles of documents, or foreign phrases that have been adopted into English.
	Example (note that **bold** is only to highlight):
	(a) We conduct the experiment not in the laboratory, but at ***Pruffeld.***
	(b) We went to **Tharandt.**
	(c) A Malawi **Kwacha** is almost 0.005 Euro.
	(d) The book published by Prof Münch in 1930 was **Stoffbewegung in Pflanzen.**
6	Biological names of genera, species, and varieties should be italicized, but not higher classifications.
	Examples:
	Family Lemnaceae
	Genera *Lemna* sp.
	Species *Lemna gibba*

4.8.8. Parentheses

Parentheses are used optionally to enclose non-restrictive or interrupting elements. The rules of the thumb guiding their use in scientific writing are as follows:

§	The rules of thumb
1	Parentheses are appropriate to enclose a non-restrictive element that is only loosely connected to the sentence and could be left out without affecting the meaning of the sentence.
2	Do not insert a parenthetical element with no relation what-so-ever to the rest of the sentence.
3	Parentheses can be used to enclose numbers in an enumeration within a

sentence.

4   When a complete sentence in parentheses comes within a sentence, it needs neither a capital letter nor a period.

Examples:

Wrong   To ascertain the role of shredders on uranium enrichment in organic partition of sediment (**Uranium** adsorb POM produced due to shredder feeding on decomposing **litter.**), *Gammarid pulex* were used in an experiment at a former uranium mining site.

Correct   To ascertain the role of shredders on uranium enrichment in organic partition of sediment (uranium adsorb POM produced due to shredder feeding on decomposing litter), *Gammarid pulex* were used in an experiment at a former uranium mining site.

5   Commas and other punctuation marks in the main sentence are always placed after the parenthesis, except in a sentence in parentheses that does not stand within another sentence. Such sentence has the end punctuation before the closing parenthesis.

Examples:

After parenthesis   In 2002 (the year of flooding in Dresden), the field sampling were irregular.

Before parenthesis   The field samplings were irregular in 2002. (This is the year Dresden experienced the worst floods in decades.)

6   Punctuation (e.g. question marks, quotation marks) of a sentence within parentheses remains within parentheses, while punctuation of the main sentence remains outside after the closing parenthesis rather than before an open parenthesis.

Example:

Wrong   The radiochemistry laboratory has gamma spectroscopy (Do they offer free)? for analysing Ra in environmental samples.

Correct   The radiochemistry laboratory has gamma spectroscopy (Do they offer free?) for analysing Ra in environmental samples.

7   A comma should precedes an open parenthesis if the parenthetical matter clearly limits the word following it.

Example:

a)   Despite being complicated, (environmental) scanning electron

> microscope is only electron microscope to characteristics the
> biomaterial changes in real operational conditions.

4.8.9. Point[14]

The point is a punctuation mark of separation. It is usually referred to as a *full stop* in British English, and a *period* in American English. Its primary purpose is to separate complete thoughts, to mark the end of declarative and imperative sentences. Exceptions are interrogative sentences, which end with a question mark, or exclamatory, which end with an exclamation point. As much as it looks obvious, the use of point is government by some rules of the thumb in scientific writing as follows:

§	Rule of the thumb
1	A point for the purpose of a punctuation mark should be used only after a sentence complete with subject and predicate.
2	A point should not be used after headings on separate lines, after running heads, after table titles, or after items in an enumerated, displayed list unless one or more of the items are complete sentences. However, run-in headings are often separated from text by a point.
3	A point should be used to end figure captions, whether or not they are complete sentences.
4	A point should follow abbreviations except those for units of measure, for acronyms, or for contractions with apostrophe.
5	A point should be used only with quotation marks, parentheses and brackets, and points of ellipsis, but not with other marks, unless the period marks an abbreviation.
6	A point should be placed before closing quotation marks.
	Example:
	Wrong The operator presses the letter n to indicate "no" and the letter y to indicate "yes".
	Right The operator presses the letter n to indicate "no" and the letter y to indicate "yes."
7	Generally points (to mark a full stop) should be placed outside closing

---

[14] The term "full stop" is by far the most common term used in British English, but it is rarely used in American English. In American English, it is called a period; the phrase "full stop" is used only in the context of transport to describe the process of completely halting the motion of a vehicle.

parentheses; a point may be placed inside only when a complete parenthetical sentence does not stand within another sentence.
Example:

a. Wrong The new project will be on iron nanoparticles as catalysers (the zero valent iron.)

    Right   The new project will be on iron nanoparticles as catalysers (the zero valent iron).

b. Wrong The new project will be on iron nanoparticles as catalysers. (The proposal has already been submitted to potential financiers).

    Right   The new project will be on iron nanoparticles as catalysers. (The proposal has already been submitted to potential financiers.)

4.8.10. Points of Ellipsis

Points of ellipsis are three evenly spaced periods (...) which are used in formal writing to indicate an omission from quoted matter. In scientific writing, point of ellipsis are usually used by peer reviewers when they suggest a correction in a manuscript. However, point of ellipsis can be used by authors. The rules of thumb guiding their use in scientific writing are as follows:

§	The rule of the thumb
1	Ellipsis points should not be used:
	Before or after a quotation run in the text;
	Before a block quotation beginning with a complete sentence; and,
	After a block quotation ending with a complete sentence.
2	Punctuation in the quote before or after the ellipsis should be retained if it will enhance meaning.

Examples:

a. Wrong "In the TU Dresden alone, hundreds of students ... scores had first class, opportunity were limited and postgraduate place suffered very competitive."

    Correct "In the TU Dresden alone, hundreds of students ..., scores had first class, opportunity were limited and postgraduate place suffered very competitive."

b. Wrong "The students were of all races and conditions ... part of the huge compost of Chinese."

Correct	"The students were of all races and conditions: ... part of the huge compost of Chinese."

3 The full stop is always retained before an ellipsis, and may be retained after ellipsis to enhance meaning

Examples:

Period before ellipsis	The size of nanoparticles is about 10 nm. ... They are produced at a very low temperature.
Period after ellipsis	The size of nanoparticles is about 10 nm because.... . They are produced at a very low temperature

4 The spacing of full stop before and after points of ellipsis may be set differently depending on best presentation of differentiation.

4.8.11. Question Mark

The purpose of the question mark is to terminate a direct question, whether the question is an independent sentence, a clause within a sentence, or a direct quotation. Here are the rules governing the use of question marks in writing, including scientific writing:

§	Rule of the thumb
1	When the direct question occurs within a sentence, the first word of the question may or may not be capitalized.

Examples:

Option 1	The question addressed by this research project is, how can the process involved in radionuclide immobilisation in sediments be influenced?
Option 2	The question addressed by this research project is, how can the process involved in radionuclide immobilisation in sediments be influenced?

2 When the question is a single word, such as when, how, or why, within a sentence, neither a question mark nor a capital is necessary, but the word is often italicized

Example:

Wrong	The article should answer the questions who? what? where? when? and, why?
Right	The article should answer the questions who, what, where,

when, and why.

3   A question mark should not follow an indirect question.
    Example:
    Wrong   The project addressed **how** process involved in radionuclide
              immobilisation in sediments can be **influenced?**
    Right   The project addressed **how** process involved in radionuclide
              immobilisation in sediments can be **influenced.**

4   The used of a question mark with other punctuation marks is guided by the
    following sub-rules:
    i.   The question mark supersedes a period or comma.
    ii.   A question mark precedes a closing quotation mark or parenthesis
          only if it is part of the quoted or parenthetical matter

          Example:
          With quotation marks   The reviewer might ask the question,
                                    What is meant by "bioefficiency"?
          With parenthesis   The obvious question is, how accurate is
                                    the model prediction (compared with
                                    experimental measurements)?

5   When a question mark does not end the sentence, a comma should never
    follow it. If required, a semicolon may follow a question mark.
    Examples:
    Comma   Wrong   The question is, how good is the model
                          prediction?, and equation (6) provides a tool for
                          answering it.
                Write   The question is, how good is the model
                          prediction? and equation (6) provides a tool for
                          answering it.
    Semicolon   The reader might well ask the question, What is meant by
                "molecular/atomic collision"?; the slash gives no clue to the
                meaning.

4.8.12. Quotation Marks

Quotation marks are used to enclose words quoted from another source, direct
discourse, or words requiring differentiation from the surrounding text. Since they
enclose, they always come in pairs. When overused, they may render a text
visually hard to read. Double quotation marks ("...") are used most of the time.

Single quotation marks ('...') are used only within double quotation marks. The general rules governing use of quotation marks for quoted material in scientific writing are as follows:

§	Rule of the thumb
1	Quotation marks should be used to enclose material taken verbatim from another source. The quote can be of any length – from a phrase to several paragraphs Examples: a. Klaus argued that sunlight was enough to demonstrate that TiO_2 was "just a super photocatalyst." b. As Jörg Schaller has explained, "The shredder produces DOC and POM which adsorb uranium from the waters.
2	Long quotations are usually set off from the text and set in a smaller type if typeset. Such block quotations should not be enclosed by quotation marks. Example: Wrong The team of researchers designing and engineering biomimetic nanostructured material wrote: "Humans have always looked to nature for design inspiration, and material design on the molecular level is no different. Here we explore how this idea applies to nanoscale biomimicry, specifically examining both recent advances and current work on engineering lipid and polymer membrane systems with cellular processes." Right The team of researchers designing and engineering biomimetic nanostructured material wrote: Humans have always looked to nature for design inspiration, and material design on the molecular level is no different. Here we explore how this idea applies to nanoscale biomimicry, specifically examining both recent advances and current work on engineering lipid and polymer membrane systems with cellular processes.
3	A word or phrase, whose meaning is being referred to, should be enclosed in quotes. Example: a. The operator presses the letter n to indicate "no" and the letter y to indicate "yes." b. The word pultruded is defined to mean the opposite of "extruded."
4	Words or phrases following entitled, the term, marked, designated,

classified, named, enclosed, cited as, referred to as, or signed should be enclosed in quotation marks, but do not enclose an expression following known as, called, or so-called unless the expression is slang.

Example:

a   The article is entitled "uranium biogeochemical dynamics in aquatic system."

b   Arsenic is classified as "carcinogenic chemical."

5 An italicized phrase or word (e.g., a title) should not be further differentiated with quotation marks.

Wrong   The article is entitled "uranium biogeochemical dynamics in aquatic system."

Right   The article is entitled "uranium biogeochemical dynamics in aquatic system."

6 Slang or technical jargon, if used, should not routinely be enclosed in quotation marks, unless it is expected to be foreign to the vocabulary of the reader. However, such terms are normally quoted only the first time they are used.

Example:

Wrong   a The SEM "captured" the biocer particles at an 70 nm.

          b The old ICP-Ms has been plutoed from analyzing certified samples.

Right   a The SEM captured the biocer particles at an 70 nm.

          b The old ICP-Ms has been "plutoed" from analyzing certified samples.

7 Coined terms or technical terms used in a non-standard way should be enclosed in quotation marks. Such terms are normally quoted only the first time they are used.

Example:

Wrong   A snapshot of the chemical speciation parameters are required.

Right   A "snapshot" of the chemical speciation parameters are required.

8 The titles of parts, likewise, sections or chapters of a report or book, and the titles of published papers, articles, etc., that are not italicized may be enclosed in quotation marks.

Example:

a   The sequential extraction procedure is described in more detail under the section entitled "Sediment Partitioning."

b   The target audience of this book is outlined in "Chapter One –

Introduction."

9 Quotation marks used with other punctuation marks follow the following regulation:

    i.   Closing quotation marks always follow commas and periods, regardless of the context.

    ii.   Closing quotation marks always precede semicolons and colons because they are always dropped at the end of quoted material.

    iii.   Closing quotation marks always follow points of ellipsis indicating omitted matter in the quote; ending a quote with ellipsis is rarely necessary.

    v   Other marks of punctuation (e.g. parentheses, question mark) are placed outside quotation marks if they are not a part of the quoted matter.

4.8.13. Semicolon

The semicolon separates coordinate clauses, long internally punctuated elements of series, explanatory phrases, and clauses, and elliptical clauses. Semicolons are usually more suitable in the longer, more complicated sentences of formal styles. In general, styles commas are often used where semicolons might appear in formal writing, or else clauses that could be linked by semicolons are written as separate sentences. However, the difference between the coma, semicolon, and a full stop is that a semicolon slows the pace and has more separating force than a comma while still tending to join clauses; a period simply separates sentences. Their uses in scientific writing are governed by the following rules of the thumb:

§	Rule of the thumb
1	When a coordinate clause is not joined by a coordinate conjunction, it must be joined by a semicolon
	Example:
	Wrong The first two experiments were treated acclimatisation only the results from last four runs were used in the analysis.
	Right The first two experiments were treated acclimatisation; only the results from last four runs were used in the analysis.
2	When coordinate clauses are joined by a coordinate conjunction but the clauses are long, complicated, or internally punctuated with commas, they may be separated by a semicolon

Example:

Not recommended	The scientists preferred the new Scanning Electron Microscope because of the less stigmatisation with biological samples, and they felt that the steadiness resulted in high resolution, focused, and contrast.
Recommended	The scientists preferred the new Scanning Electron Microscope because of the less stigmatisation with biological samples; and they felt that the steadiness resulted in high resolution, focused and contrast.

3 When coordinate clauses are joined by a conjunctive adverb (e.g. however, thus, therefore, hence), a semicolon must precede the conjunctive adverb.

Example:

Wrong	Phosphates generally reduced the uptake of arsenate by aquatic macrophyte, however, phosphate increased the total accumulation when the macrophytes had iron plaques.
Right	Phosphates generally reduced the uptake of arsenate by aquatic macrophyte; however, phosphate increased the total accumulation when the macrophytes had iron plaques

4 The semicolon is particularly effective between contrasting clauses.

Example:

Wrong	One antibody performed slightly better with the transfection of nanodiamond, the other antibody performed much worse.
Right	One antibody performed slightly better with the transfection of nanodiamond; the other antibody performed much worse.

5 To improve clarity when elements of a series are long, complex, or internally punctuated with commas, semicolons may be used.

Example:

Wrong	The constituents of the Hutner medium are NH_4NO_3, $CaCl_2$, $MgSO_4$, KH_2PO_4; EDTA, KOH, H_3BO_3, $ZnSO_4 \cdot 7H_2O$, $CaCl_2 \cdot 2H_2O$, $MnCl_2 \cdot 4H_2O$, $(NH_4)_6MO_7O_{24} \cdot 4H_2O$, and $COCl_2 \cdot 6H_2O$, $CuSO_4 \cdot 5H_2O$, $FeSO_4 \cdot 7H_2O$.
Right	The constituents of the Hutner medium are NH_4NO_3, $CaCl_2$, $MgSO_4$, KH_2PO_4; EDTA, KOH, H_3BO_3, $ZnSO_4 \cdot 7H_2O$, $CaCl_2 \cdot 2H_2O$, $MnCl_2 \cdot 4H_2O$, $(NH_4)_6MO_7O_{24} \cdot 4H_2O$; and $COCl_2 \cdot 6H_2O$, $CuSO_4 \cdot 5H_2O$, $FeSO_4 \cdot 7H_2O$.

6 When explanatory information follows introductory phrase like that is, namely, for example, in other words, for instance, a semicolon must

precede the phrase when it introduces an independent clause.

Example:

Wrong   Some random processes are reasonably independent of the precise time, that is, measurements made at different times are similar in their average properties.

Right   Some random processes are reasonably independent of the precise **time; that** is, measurements made at different times are similar in their average properties.

7   A semicolon should be used to separate elliptical clauses when commas are necessary to indicate the omission in an elliptical construction.

Example:

Wrong   Radionuclide concentration was analyzed with ICP-MS, structure of the crystals, with X-ray defractometer, and radiation, with gammaspectoscopy.

Right   Radionuclide concentration was analysed with ICP-MS; structure of the crystals, with X-ray defractometer; and radiation, with gammaspectoscopy.

8   If a comma is unnecessary to indicate omission, the semicolon can be replaced by a comma as long as the clauses are joined by a conjunction.

Example:

With semicolon   Wind speed is obtained from antenna brightness temperature; wind vector, from radar cross section.

With Comma   Wind speed is obtained from antenna brightness temperature, and wind vector from radar cross section.

4.8.14. Slash

Use of a slash is rarely acknowledged in grammar, likewise in scientific writing, except in fractions (e.g. x/y) and to indicate "per" (e.g. m/sec, g/L); otherwise, a hyphen is preferred to a slash. However, some technical terms have become standard with the slash. Thus, only terms that is accepted as standard with a slash may be used with the slash in scientific writing.

4.8.15. Capitalization

Due to differences in capitalization rules between German and English, most German scientific writers face a major problem in deciding which words or part of a sentence to capitalize. In German, all nouns start with a capital letter, while in English, there are several rules in which nouns should be capitalized. However, the rules fail to cover every conceivable problem in capitalization in scientific writing, except for rules from English grammar. Actually, capitalization in scientific writing covers more than what is provided in English grammar because some capitalizations are a matter of editorial style and preference rather than a matter of generally accepted rules. There is so much difference of opinion concerning capitalization of words in a document that total. Therefore, an important goal for scientific writers should be consistency within a particular document. However, there are clear-cut rules on capitalization, which are introduced below. For details, McCaskill [62] has provided a best guideline on capitalization, which is worth reading. There are three ways of capitalizing [62], *vis a vis*:

1. Full caps, which means that every letter in an expression is a capital (e.g., URANIUM DECAY PROCESS);
2. Caps and lower case, which means that the principal words of an expression are capitalized (e.g., Phosphate Regulates Uranium Toxicity); and
3. Caps and small caps, which refers to a particular font type containing small capital letters instead of lowercase letters (e.g. FATE AND EFFECT OF URANIUM IN AQUATIC SYSTEM).

Rules of the Thumb on Capitalization

Some of the rules of thumb to assist in deciding where and which words or part of a sentence should be capitalized are as follows:

§	Rules of the thumb
1	The first word in a sentence is ordinarily capitalized, except in a sentence enclosed in parentheses within another sentence. However, a parenthesized sentence that does not stand within another sentence should also start with a capital letter.

Example:

a. Plant samples for arsenic preparation are freeze-dried (the freeze-drying is preferred because methylarsenic species are volatile at temperature above 30 °C), a procedure critical for heavy metal determination with ICP-MS.

b.   Plant samples for arsenic preparation are freeze-dried. (The freeze-drying procedure is preferred because methylarsenic species are volatile at temperature above 30 °C). It is a procedure critical for heavy metal determination with ICP-MS.

2   Capitalization of a complete sentence after a colon is optional. However, the first word after a colon may be capitalized when the capital begins a complete sentence.

Example:

Correct	The speciation of uranium is pH dependent in aquatic system: At pH 6, free uranium ions dominates.
Equally	The speciation of uranium is pH dependent in aquatic system: at pH 6, free uranium ions dominates.

3   A direct quotation that is not syntactically joined to the rest of the sentence (often set off by commas) should begin with a capital, even if the initial letter is not a capital in the source.

Example:

Wrong	In the thermodynamics, the gas law states: "In an ideal state of any gas, a given number of its particles occupy the same volume, and volume changes are inverse to pressure changes and linear to temperature changes."
Correct	In the thermodynamics, the gas law states: "In an ideal state of any gas, a given number of its particles occupy the same volume, and volume changes are inverse to pressure changes and linear to temperature changes."

4   When the quote is syntactically dependent on the rest of the sentence, it begins with a lowercase letter, even if the initial letter is capital in the source.

Example:

Wrong	The Institute of Materials Science established the Max Bergmann Centre in 2002 "To take a leading role in biomaterial research and bionanotechnology."
Correct	The Institute of Material Sciences established the Max Bergmann Centre in 2002 "to take a leading role in biomaterial research and bionanotechnology."

5   The first word when a direct question occurs within a sentence is optionally capitalized. However, an indirect question should never be capitalized.

Example:

Direct   a.   The question addressed by this research project is, What processes are involve in biomineralisation of arsenic?

                b.   The question addressed by this research project is, what processes are involve in biomineralisation of arsenic?

Indirect   This research project addressed what processes are involved in biomineralisation of arsenic.

6   All items in a displayed list should begin with a capital, whether they are complete sentences or not. When items are not in a list, they should never be capitalized.

Examples:

List   The objectives of the study are:
                1. To test feasibility of biocer-based bioreactor; and
                2. To verify the biodegradation in a flowing system.

Non-list   The objectives of the study are (1) to test feasibility of biocer-based bioreactor; and (2) to verify the biodegradation in a flowing system.

7   Acronyms should always be formed with capitals unless the acronym stands for a proper name.

8   Words that have crept into the languages, but initially acronyms, should not be capitalized[15].

Examples:

a)   laser   **L**ight **A**mplification by **S**timulated **E**mission of **R**adiation
b)   radar   **R**adio **D**etection **and R**anging

9   An abbreviation should follow the capitalization of the word or words abbreviated [62], *vis* lowercase abbreviations should always be left lowercase, particularly abbreviations for units of measure.

10   In general, proper nouns and derivatives of proper nouns used in a proper sense should be capitalized. However, derivatives of proper nouns that have acquired an independent meaning are not capitalized.

Example:

---

[15] The difference between abbreviations and acronyms :
1.   An abbreviation is a shortened version of a word or phrase and is often followed by a point, for example, c.o.d., St., or publ. Most abbreviations have become standard so that their form can be looked up in reference books.
2.   Acronyms, on the other hand, are words formed from the initial letters of successive parts of a term, for example, SEM, Laser, UV, Rader, DAAD. They never contain periods and are often not standard, so that definition is required.

a)   Rome, Roman, roman numerals

11   When a word the is part of an official name, it should be capitalized.
Example:

a)   The Institute of General Ecology and Environmental Protection

b)   The Max Bergman Centre for Biomaterial

12   In non-English personal names, particles such as d', de, du, and von, are capitalized, unless preceded by a forename or title.

Examples:

a)   Dr. Hans von Mende

b)   Dr. Von Mende

13   A personal name that is used in common sense, especially as a unit, should not be capitalized except where the personal name is used to qualify the units.
Examples:

Not capitalized	Curie, watt, newton, and Kelvin
Capitalised	degree Celsius
	degree Rankine
	degree Fahrenheit

14   Civil and professional titles are capitalized when they precede a personal name as part of the name; however, such titles are not capitalized in apposition.
Examples:

	Capitalized	Not capitalized
a.	President Chizi	the president, Mr. Chizi
b.	Director Chimango	the director, Ms Chimango
c.	Chief Scientist Msau	the chief scientist, Ms Msau
d.	Editor-in-Chief Martin	the editor-in-chief, Martin

15   In a document to a very specific audience, a common noun used as part of or in place of a personal name may be capitalized.
Examples:

a.   The Editor

b.   The Professor

16   Names of months and days of the week, various holidays, historic events, and other time designations are capitalized, but seasons and time zones are not capitalized.
Examples:

Wrong	a.	january, tuesday, christmas day, unification day.
	b.	Summer, Winter, Spring, Autumn

Correct	a.	January, Tuesday, Christmas day, Unification-day.
	b.	summer, winter, spring, autumn

17   Directions of the compass are capitalized only as a part of a name that has been established by usage to designate particular regions

Examples:

Wrong	a.	south Africa
	b.	West Africa
Right	a.	South Africa
	b.	west Africa

18   The names of particular regions, localities, countries, and geographic features are capitalized.

Examples:

Geographic features	Northern Hemisphere, Southern Hemisphere, Arctic Circle, North Pole, Equator, Tropic of Cancer, etc.
Regions and localities	Sub-Saharan Africa, Middle East, South Asia, etc
Physical features	(i.e. rivers, mountains and cities) Elbe River, Mount Everest, etc

19   There are conventions for capitalization of names in several scientific disciplines, for instance in biologic taxonomy. The names at phylum, class, order, family, and genus levels should be capitalized, but species level should not be capitalized.

4.9. Clearing Fog of Formula

A particular kind of technical density that can be especially intimidating is an unbroken chain of mathematical formula. Many scientists and engineers believe that technical ideas are best communicated in the rigor of mathematical formulas. Many people believe that they are making a point more clearly and precisely by translating it into mathematical symbols. This seldom happens. There are moments when scientific ideas, which are full of mathematical formulas, can be communicated without any formula. There are also instances where mathematical formulas are unavoidable and the linguistic shortcuts in the scientific writing. However, when laying out pages of solid mathematics, no matter how profound, it ends up with technical density, which is usually difficult to understand unless one is a mathematician.

Therefore, a decision to present the report in mathematical or normal text language should be examined consciously. The original reason for using mathematical formula was to make things clearer, not more obscure. Thus, when deciding whether to present an idea in text or in mathematical formulas, the authors should examine what would be likely to enhance the communication with your audience, and what would be likely to obscure it. If a subject has a high concentration of mathematical symbols and formulas, the following questions should be answered about each formula before putting them into the manuscript:

#	Question
1.	Is it necessary to express this idea in a mathematical symbols, or could a point have been made more clearly using text?
2.	Does the formula contribute to the mainstream logic of the paper, or is it just a detour in a mathematical derivation that could be in an appendix?

Once it is decided that mathematical symbols or formulas would best communicate the scientific discourse, the following rules of thumb should guide their application in scientific writing:

§	Rule of the thumb
1	All symbols appearing in the manuscript should be adequately defined;
2	The significance of each mathematical step in the development of your paper should be explained clearly;
3	If there are many mathematical formulas, at least an equal weight of text should be put to balance out the mathematics. Thus, some explanations introduced by phrases (e.g. in other words …; what this means is …; for example …; that is …) should be inserted between formulas;
4	Make sure that mathematical symbols are linguistic shortcuts whose meanings are universally agreed upon.

4.10. CHAPTER COMPENDIUM

"We all learn to read more difficult words before we understand them!" True! However, good writing should proceed regularly from things known to things unknown, distinctly and clearly without confusion. The words used should be the most expressive that the language affords, and most generally understood. Good writing demands that nothing should be expressed in two words that can be as well expressed in one; that is, no synonyms should be used, or very rarely, but the whole should be as short as possible, consistent with clearness; and the words should be so placed as to be agreeable to the ear in reading. In short, good writing is demonstrated when the writing is smooth, clear, and short.

As far as scientific and academic writing is concerned, authors should write in a manner that is accessible to their readership. Most readers are not native-speakers of English, though they are generally well read in the subject area. Others who are native-speakers of English may be new to the diverse fields of environmental sciences, technology, and engineering. These facts should not lead to simplify your content, rather, they mean writing should be straightforward and direct. Therefore, two critical questions to ask about readability are:

(a) What is readable academic writing? and,
(b) How can researchers write readably?

For good readability, the following rules of the thumb help:

§   **Rules of the thumb**
1. Average sentence length should be 13 to 17 words. Occasional longer sentences are okay, but an average length beyond 17 words will weary the reader. It will be hard to read and understand.
2. A scientific writing should not have more than 10 percent passive sentences. Active verbs put action into words. The active voice gives meaning to the reader.
3. Learning correct punctuation is a must because it helps reduce fog in the writing.
4. ESL writers should avoid translating the text directly from their first language because they are attempting to translate word-by-word. Such word-by-word translations bring a lot of fog in writing. Hence, it is advisable to write directly in English.
5. Authors have the opportunity to improve their own writing by rewriting sentences and paragraphs, and by reviewing their own writing and that of other participants.
6. Scientific and mathematic formulas are not a justification for presenting articles that are difficult to read.

Finally, this chapter looked at how to increase readability in the scientific writing. It does not teach a particular type of report writing. The chapter does not teach the rules of grammar. The rules of English grammar are extensive and comprehensive and out of the scope of this book. The chapter only provides tips on fogless sentence structure by focusing on the differences between independent and dependent clauses. These aspects are then used to review the basic rules of correct punctuation.

The examples and ideas included in this chapter come from observations on manuscripts I peer-reviewed for some high impact international journal. What I learned was many people are productive writers but they still struggle with a range of different writing problems – the most important ones are: (a) difficulty with writing down their thoughts; (b) punctuation; (c) getting their point across; (d) writing succinctly; (e) structuring their documents; (f) writing clear paragraphs; and, (g) knowing what writing rules to follow and what rules to use as a guide in different circumstances.

Chapter 5

HOW TO CONQUER FLAWS?

Brian [63] defines errors in English as deviations from the standard use of English as judged by sophisticated users such as professional writers, editors, teachers, literate executives, and personnel officers. This definition also covers almost everything that can be considered a flaw in scientific writing. However, flaws in scientific writing might not be mistakes in Standard English *vis* language and grammar. Further flaws in scientific writing have very distinct borders of definition within a particular scientific field. For instance, what may be regarded as a scientific writing error in one field, like pure chemistry, it may not necessarily be an error in other fields like applied chemistry, psychology, or medicine [38, 39, 44, 46]. On the contrary, errors in English language and grammar are errors in all scientific writing.

The errors in writing scientific work in English differ according to the characteristics of their first languages [63]. Scientific writers, whose first languages are not English, tend to make some specific errors that are uncommon among native speakers. However, when one reads articles or books on common mistakes in English, most of the mistakes seem to be universal without necessarily being confined to ESL speaking scientists only. In this chapter, I list common errors and flaws committed by scientist in their writing projects. I came across these errors (1) during proofreading manuscripts from colleagues, (2) assisting some international postgraduate student writing their thesis in English, and (3) peer-reviewing a number of manuscripts for a number of international journals in the field of environmental sciences, engineering, and technology.

5.1. HOW TO AVOID PLAGIARISM

There is a growing tendency to run away from the trouble of writing one's own ideas and passing off someone else's writing (or other intellectual work) as one's own. Many borrowed ideas and writing are being passed without acknowledging to the owners. This problem is not only common among ESL or novice in scientific writing, but also with native English and professional writers.. Unfortunately, as already described, this is plagiarism, which is theft and fraud, and constitute to a crime [15, 16, 24, 26-29, 31].

Even the best writers are often unaware of their good ideas and think they have nothing to say when their writing says a lot [13, 27]. Original ideas come from working closely with the ideas of others, not from flashes of inspiration [12-16, 27]. As already described, this is plagiarism, which is theft and fraud, and constitute to a crime [15, 16, 24, 26-29, 31]. The advent of the internet has provided a very big and easy opportunity for plagiarism. Since any file on the internet can be downloaded as a text file, these papers can be copied by anyone who gains access to them [25, 28, 29, 31]. Many people easily download already written and typed documents and make a few changes, or sometimes just cut and paste from different documents to suit their own document.

By using sources well and by clearly indicating the debts to these sources, one's writing gains authority, clarity, and precision [8, 11, 24, 26, 28]. Writers cannot hope to indicate or even be aware of all their borrowings, and there is a point where an idea borrowed from someone else becomes one's own after long reflection [12, 24, 26, 28]. So long as writers are scrupulous about indicating material they have borrowed in paraphrases, authors are not be suspected or guilty of plagiarism. Avoiding plagiarism is an important matter of personal, academic, and professional ethics. Plagiarism can be avoided by carefully following these rules of the thumb [24, 26-31, 64]:

§   **Rules of the thumb**
1   Authors should give themselves plenty of time to research and write so that they could have time to digest the work of others. During this time, authors should take research notes that include full bibliographic citations. This ensures that writers easily cite a source when they prepare the manuscript.
2   Avoid working directly from the source material (e.g. editing a cut and pasted material), because working directly from the work or editing the work can easily lead a mosaic plagiarism. Originality comes from synthesizing what has been read from works of others.

3   Quotation, where the exact words or text spoken or written should be reproduced exactly, and they should be enclosed either within quotation marks or in the case of a longer passage; they should be indented as a distinct block of text.   Follow or introduce such a clearly marked quotation with information on where the words or text originate.

4   Just substituting synonyms for some of the words is not enough when summarizing or paraphrasing an idea read or spoken elsewhere.   The ideas must be digested, understood, and re-written in one's own words and sentence patterns.   Nevertheless, the source must still be identified and acknowledged, because even though the words and sentence patterns are the authors original, the ideas are not.

5   Sources of facts or statistics should generally be identified and acknowledged except for common knowledge, such as the fact that uranium is a number 92nd element in the periodic table.

6   Sources of ideas, material, and information obtained from the internet including material from Web pages, e-mail, and newsgroups should be cited.

5.2. FLAWS INFLUENCED BY FIRST LANGUAGE – A CASE OF GERMAN AS A FIRST LANGUAGE

Most of the Indo-Germanic[1] languages have a lot of similarity.   A good example is German and English.   German is very close to English in vocabulary because they share the same Latin root, but they are very different in grammar. Sometimes, the sentence may be grammatically correct while logically wrong. There is no standard approach to avoiding such mistakes apart from reading and speaking from which special words and sentence construction can be observed. Here are some common and typical errors of writers I came across while proofreading works of colleagues whose first language is German – some of the errors were also common in manuscripts from other ESL contributors (including non-Indo-Germanic), which I peer reviewed:

---

[1] Family of several hundred related languages and dialects, including most of the major languages of Europe, the northern Indian subcontinent, Southwest Asia, and much of Central Asia. They are descended from a single unrecorded language believed to have been spoken more than 5,000 years ago in the steppe regions north of the Black Sea and to have split into a number of dialects by 3000 BC.   Some of the contemporary languages are: Italian, English, Hindi, Portuguese, Bengali, Russian, Spanish, German, Marathi, French, Punjabi and Urdu.

(i) Flaws due to Adoption of German Sentence Construction

Many mistakes in construction are due to literal translation form the native language, German to English are visible with the following:

(a) Placement of action verbs at the end of the sentence when the sentence contains an auxiliary is a sentence construction rule applied in German. However, adopting the same rule for English sentence construction is wrong. Unless otherwise noted, the action verb should be placed immediately after the auxiliary verb in English sentence construction.

Examples:

Wrong	The uranium has been today on the ICP-MS measured.
Correct	The uranium has been measured today on the ICP-MS.

(b) Excessive use of "has been" and "have" in stead of using direct past or present tense because it is common and accepted to use past perfect for simple past tense in German language where auxiliary verb "haven" is used.

Examples:

Wrong	a	The MTBE have been determined with gas chromatography.
	b	We have measured MTBE with gas chromatography
Correct	a	The MTBE was measured with gas chromatography
	b	We measured MTBE with gas chromatography.

(c) Frequent placing of indirect object clause in front of the sentence is common when German speakers write in English. This may be attributed to the absence of noun declination in English. In most Indo-Germanic languages, the direct or indirect objects (accusative or dative) are determined by declination and not position, like in English.

Examples:

Wrong	With aqua regia in microwave digesters, the sediment samples were digested before metal analysis on IOC-PMS.
Correct	The sediment samples were digested with aqua regia in microwave digesters before metal analysis on IOC-PMS.

(ii) Flaws due to Literal Translation of Words Form German to English

(a) Translation of German combined words (*Zusammenworte*) as English idioms

Examples:

I	"Überleben" means "survive" and not "over live"
	Wrong Lemna gibba can over live the winter in tailing ponds.
	Correct Lemna gibba can survive the winter in tailing ponds.
Ii	"Überarbeiten" (German) means "revise" (English) and not "over work"
	Wrong I have over worked the poster for the conference in Madrid .
	Correct I have revised the poster for the conference in Madrid.
Iii	Fahren (German) can mean drive, or travel. Hence, mistakes rise in interchanging the English translation.
	Wrong You can drive by train from Schönefeld Airport to Dresden.
	Correct You can come/use/travel by train from Schönefeld Airport to Dresden.

(b)   (i) Translation of verbs and nouns ending in "ieren" and "ierung" respectively.

Examples:

German	English translation	
	Wrong	**Correct**
automatisierung	automatation	automatisation
mobisierung	mobisitation	mobilisation
solubisierung	solubisitation	dissolution

(ii) Verb form of nouns ending "-cation" and "-bility"

Examples

Noun		Verb	
		Wrong	**Correct**
a	application	applicate	apply
b	modification	modificate	modify

| c | separation | seperatise | separate |
| d | solubility | solubilise | dissolve |

(c) Similar word, different meanings

Many words may be the same in English and Germany but their meanings are totally different.

Examples

| Wrong | The immigration officer controlled my passport. |
| Correct | The immigration officer checked my passport. |

(d) Words with similar meaning but different in their use in German and English.

Examples:

(i) Personnen

The word "persons" is hardly used in spoken English, but only in a legal context (e.g. sign on a lift: Max 12 Persons)

German		Wir sind vier Leute
English	Wrong	We are four persons.
	Correct	There are four of us.

(ii) Seit

Use of "Seit" in German is similar to use of both "for" and "since" in English. Below are some regulations of when to use "since" or "for" in English when translating a sentence containing "seit" from German to English.

	Wrong	Correct
1	I am married since five years.	I have been married for five years.
2	We have had the project for January 2006.	We have had the project since January 2006.

(iii) Seite

Seite means "side" in English. However, it is mostly used in an expression "an eine seite … und an andere seite ist …" equivalent to "on one side … and on the other …". Specific to note is that in Germany "seite" is used twice, while English it is "one" and then "other".

Examples:

Wrong	On the one side, there are some disadvantages, on the other side, there are many advantages.
Correct	On the one side, there are some disadvantages, while on the other, there are many advantages.

(e) Confusion with the use of translation of prepositions.

(i) "Bei" in German sound the same as the preposition "by" in English. However, their uses are not the same, as "bei" is used sometimes as the English "with" to indication possession.

Examples:

Wrong	The book is by John.
Correct	The book is with John.

(ii) "Mit", when expressed with an age, should not be translated as "with" in English.

Examples:

Wrong	With 23, I started my training.
Correct	At (the age of) 23, I started my training.

(h) Translating the German plural into irregular nouns in English.

Examples:
(i) Informationen
Information in English is an irregular noun in that its singular and plural form is the same, while in German it has plural "*informationen*".

Usage:

Wrong:	Please send me the informations.
Correct:	Please send me the information.

(ii) Percentage
Percentage is never plural in English, while in German it is always plural.

Example of usage in English:

Wrong	10% are very high.

Correct	10% is very high.

(i)   Single word in German for two words in English.

Examples:

(i)   "Lehnen" in German can be translated as "to learn" and "to study". However, they are used differently.

Examples:

(a) "lennen" for "studying"

Wrong	I am learning for chemistry examination on Monday.
Correct	I am studying for chemistry examination on Monday.

(b) "lennen" for "learning"

Wrong	I am studying to write in school.
Correct	I am learning to write in school.

(ii) "Sagen" in German means either "to say" or "to tell".

Examples:

(a) "sagen" for "to tell"

Wrong	Please, say me when you are ready.
Correct	Please, tell me when you are ready.

(b) "sagen" for "to say"

Wrong	He was telling in class that uranium is less toxic than arsenic.
Correct	He was saying in class that uranium is less toxic than arsenic.

(iii) "Entschludigung" can mean either "sorry (for apologize) or "excuse me".

Examples:

(a) "entschludigung" for "excuse me"

Wrong	Sorry, may I pass.
Correct	Excuse me, may I pass.

(b) "entschludigung" for "sorry"
  (i)   I am sorry for what I did.
  (ii) Excuse me for what I did.

(iv) "Ausleien, ausborgen" can be either borrow or lend.

Examples:

Wrong	Could you borrow me your book?
	I have borrowed my pencil to Arndt.
Correct	Can you lend me your book?
	I have lent my pencil to Arndt.

(v) "Hören" is translated as "to hear" or "to listen" in English.

Examples:

Wrong	(a)	He is hearing to music.
	(b)	He listened the warning, but he could not simply run away.
Correct	(a)	He is listening to music.
	(b)	He heard the warning, but he could not simply run away.

(g) Transtlation and use of some specific words.

(i) "haben"

The verb "haben" can be translated to "have" in English, but when it is literally translated into English, it is sometimes wrong. Use of the verb "haben" (German) as auxiliary can be alternated to "to be" and wrongly translate to "have" (English).

Examples:

Wrong	Today, we have 20 degree Celsius.
Correct	Today, it (the temperature) is 20 degrees Celsius.

(ii) Junge (in context of time)

In German, "among others' indicates when an event took place. Unfortunately, literal translation into English means young, which cannot be used in the context of the latest.

Examples:

Wrong	Please, submit your youngest resume.
Correct	Please, submit your most recent resume.

(iii) Use of the translation of "nächste mal".

Literal translation of this expression should never be used in English.

Examples:

Wrong	I will look at it in the next time.
Correct	I will look at it in the coming weeks.

(iv) Tall

In German, there is no explicit expression translation of "tall". The word used is "gross there", which means big. As a result, Germans have a tendency of using "long" or "big" to describe the height of a person.

Example:

Wrong	He is very long.
Correct	He is very tall.

(iii) Use of Reflexive Verbs

German has unique reflexive construction verbs. Such construction hardly exists in English. Literal translation and use of such reflexive verb constructions are errors in English.

Examples:

(i)	Treffen uns (German) is not the same as meet us (English)	
	Wrong	We meet us tomorrow.
	Correct	We will meet tomorrow;
		Or, We will meet tomorrow?
(ii)	Uns sehen (German) is not the same as see us (English).	
	Wrong	We will see us tomorrow.
	Correct	I will see you tomorrow.
(iii)	Mich kaufen (German) in not buy me (English).	
	Wrong	I bought me a computer for 900 €uro.
	Correct	I bought a computer for 900 €uro.
(iv)	mich bedanken (in German) in not thank me (in English).	
	Wrong	I thank us for the assistance.
	Correct	I thank you for the assistance.

5.3. COMMONLY CONFUSED WORDS

This section presents some of words most commonly confused in most manuscripts I reviewed or proofread, regardless of either EFL or ESL submission; however, the tendency was more among the ESL contributors. Thus, this indicates that most of the mistakes may not necessary be those influenced by being non-native English language speakers, but by generally being confusing words, either due to their spelling or pronunciation, or having similar meanings, but not being the same. The list here is not exhaustive because it lists only the mistakes that this author came across. There are a number of publications devoted to common errors in English which can be accessed in books, journal articles, and electronics on the internet (See further reading and bibliography section).

Examples:

principal vs. Principle
> Principal is an adjective, meaning something important;
> Principle is a noun, meaning some underlying law or assumption.
> Examples:
> Principle   The principal step in the proof...
> principal   The principle of induction ...

accept vs. Except
> Accept is a verb, which means to agree to take something.
> Except is a preposition or conjunction, which means not including.
> Examples:
> accept   I always accept good advice.
> except   I teach every day except Sundays.

advice vs. Advise
> Advice is a noun, which means an opinion that someone offers you about what you should do or how you should act in a particular situation.
> Advise is a verb, which means to give information and suggest types of action.
>
> Examples:
> Advice   I need someone to give me some advice.
> Advise   I advise everybody to be nice to his or her teacher.

although vs. Though

Although begins a clause, both at the beginning and in the middle of a sentence.

Though is used as a synonym for "however."

Note: Although and though are technically interchangeable.

Examples:

Though   (i)   Though no example has been found, ...

              (ii)   No example has been found, though.

Although   Although no example has been found, ...

affect vs. Effect

Affect is usually an action verb and it means to influence, act upon, or change something or someone.

Effect is usually a noun which is followed by the preposition on and preceded by an article (an, the), and means to have an impact on something or someone. Effect can also mean "the end result".

Hint: If it is something, you are going to do, use "affect." If it is something you have already done, use "effect".

Examples:

Affect   The noise outside affected my performance.

Effect   (i)   The drug has many adverse side effects.

              (ii)   His smile had a strange effect on me.

a lot vs. alot vs. Allot

A lot can be used to modify a noun, meaning a large amount or number of people or things. It can also be used as an adverb, meaning very much or very often.

Alot does not exist. There is no such word in the English language.

Allot is a verb, which means to give (especially a share of something) for a particular purpose.

Examples:

A lot   (i)   I need a lot of time to develop this web site.

              (ii)   I look a lot like my sister.

Allot   We were allotted a desk each.

all ready vs. Already

All ready means "completely ready".

Already is an adverb" that means before the present time or earlier than the time expected.

Examples

All ready	Are you all ready for the test?
Already	(i) I asked him to come to the cinema but he had already seen the film.
	(ii) Are you buying Christmas cards already? It's only September!

altogether vs. all together

All together (adv) means "together in a single group".

Altogether (adv) means "completely" or "in total".

Examples:

All together	The waiter asked if we were all together.
Altogether	She wrote less and less often, and eventually she stopped altogether.

apart vs. a part

Apart is an adverb, which means separated by distance or time.

A part is a noun, which means a piece of something that forms the whole of something.

Examples:

Apart	I always feel so lonely when we are apart.
A part	They made me feel like I was a part of the family.

been vs. Gone

Been is the past participle of be. It is used to describe completed visits.

gone is the past participle of go

Examples:

Been	If you have been to Heidelberg twice, you have travelled there and back twice.
Gone	If you have gone to Heidelberg, you have not yet returned.

bored vs. Boring

Bored is an adjective that describes when someone feels tired and unhappy because something is not interesting or because they have nothing to do.

Boring is an adjective that means something is not interesting or exciting.

Note: Most verbs, which express emotions, such as to bore, may use either the present or the past participle as an adjective, but the meaning of the participles is often different.

Examples:

Bored	She was so bored that she fell asleep.
Boring	The lesson was so boring that she fell asleep.

borrow vs. Lend

Borrow is to take with permission usually for a certain length of time.
Lend is to hand out usually for a certain length of time.

Examples

Borrow	I will borrow the manuscript from Peter.
Lend	I lend my manuscript to Peter.

bought vs. Brought

Bought is past tense of the verb to buy.
Brought is past tense of the verb to bring.

Examples:

Bought	I bought a pair of sport shoes from Peter.
Brought	Chizi brought his homework to the party.

by vs. Until

Until indicates how long a situation continues. It can also be used in negatives statements.
By indicates something happens at or before a particular time. It is often used to indicate a deadline.

Examples:

Until	a.	The project report will not be available until January.
	b.	The uranium speciation project ran until September.
By		You have to finish the thesis by August.

complement vs. Compliment

Complement is a verb, which means to make something seem better or more attractive when combined.
Compliment is a noun, which means a remark that expresses approval, admiration or respect.

Examples:

Complement	The colors blue and green complement each other perfectly.

| Compliment | I am often complimented on this web site. |

do have to vs. must

Do have to indicates that there is obligation or necessity to do something. Must is a modal verb used to show that something is allowed. Likewise, "must not" tells people not to do things. It has the same force as do not, as in: Do not do that!

Examples:

Do have to	You do not have to do the exercises at the end of this page.
Must	a. You must not drink and drive.
	b. You must finish your home work before going to play.

during vs. while

During is for use with nouns.
While is for use with verbs.

Examples:

| During | I fell asleep during the meeting. |
| While | I fell asleep while I was driving. |

deny vs. refuse

Deny mean to refuse to admit the existence, truth, or value (e.g. denied the rumour, contradicted the statement, contravene a conclusion, disaffirm a suggestion, negated the allegations, and traverse an indictment).

Refuse means to be unwilling to accept, consider, or receive someone or something. Refuse usually implies determination and often brusqueness.

Examples:

Deny	i. The protesters were denied audience with the minister.
	ii. He denies her weekly allowance.
Refuse	i. The commander refused to discuss questions of right.
	ii. We will make an offer, which he cannot refuse.

date vs. appointment

Date is between people in a love affair – a befriend with a girlfriend or wife with husband and vice versa;

Appointment is between people at business level and not relationship.

Examples:

Date	John has a date with Mary at 21:00.
Appointment	I have an appointment with my scientific supervisor.

either vs. Too

Either is used with a negative verb when you are agreeing with something someone does not do or like etc.

Too is used with an affirmative verb when you are agreeing with something someone does or likes etc.

Examples:

Either   Carsten agrees with Kerstin in the negative:

(i) Carsten says, "I don't like cheese". Kerstin replies "I don't like it either".

(ii) Carsten says "I haven't seen Lord of the Rings". Kerstin replies "I haven't seen it either".

Too   Arndt agrees with Karin in the positive:

(i) Karin says "I love ice-cream". Arndt replies "I love it too".

(ii) Karin says "I've seen Gladiator". Arndt replies, "I've seen it too".

every day vs. Everyday

Every day is a determiner and day is a noun. When one says every day, he or she means each day without exception.

Everyday means ordinary and unremarkable. Everyday is an adjective.

Examples:

Every day	He records the research data at 10 O'clock every day.
Everyday	My book offers an insight into the everyday life of Dresden.

fewer vs. Less

Fewer is used for things you can count (individually). It has to do with how many.

Less for things, one can only measure. It has to do with how much.

Examples:

Fewer	There were fewer days below freezing last winter. (Days can be counted.)
Less	I drink less coffee than Burckhardt does. (Coffee cannot be counted individually it has to be measured).

farther vs. further

Farther indicates physical to distance.

Further indicate a continuation or extension in terms of time, degree, or anything else other than distance.

They are both a comparative form of "far".

Examples:

Farther	He went farther than milestones set in the initial project document.
Further	(i) He is doing further education.
	(ii) Further to our discussion, I would like to confirm my coming.

for vs. Since

For indicates a period.

Since indicates a point in time.

Examples:

For	The experiment has been running for 2 years.
Since	The experiment has been running since 1995.

I vs. *Me*

I is a subject form.

Me is an object form.

Examples:

I	I am a scientist.
Me	(i) Give that to me.
	(ii) The reviewer forwarded the criticism on the manuscript to me.

interested vs. interesting

Interested is a past participle. When used as an adjective, it says how someone feels.

Interesting is a present participle. When used as an adjective, it describes the people or things that cause the feelings.

Examples:

Interested	I was very interested in the lesson.
Interesting	It was an interesting lesson.

lay vs. Lie

Lay is an irregular transitive verb (lay / laid/ laid - laying). It needs a direct object. It means to put something or someone down (often in a horizontal position).

Lie is an irregular intransitive verb (lie / lay / lain - lying). It does not take a direct object. It means to rest in a horizontal position or to be located somewhere.

Note: The past tense of "lie" is "lay".

Lie also means to say something that is not true but it takes the following form (lie / lied / lied - lying).

Examples:

Lay	(i)	Lay your head on the pillow.
	(ii)	Dresden lies in the Midlands.
Lie	(i)	If you are tired, lie down and have a rest.
	(ii)	He lied about his inappropriate affair to the grand jury.

look after vs. look for

Look after means to take care of or be in charge of something or someone.

Look for means to try to find something or someone.

Examples:

| Look after | We usually ask Paul to look after the children. |
| Look for | I am looking for my keys. Have you seen them? |

look vs. Watch

Look is usually followed by the preposition at. When one looks at someone or something, (s)he is interested in the appearance. Generally, one looks at things that are static.

Watch is not followed by a preposition. When one watches someone or something, (s)he is interested in what happens. Generally, one watches things that move or change state.

If one says "Look at him!", it mean check out his appearance.

If one says "Watch him!", it check what the person is doing (i.e. it is a warning).

Examples:

Look	(i)	Look at these pictured from scanning electron microscopes, they are good.
	(ii)	I went to the conference hall to look at the exhibition of posters.
Watch	(i)	I watch TV every night.
	(ii)	The security guard watched the shoplifter steal the

clock.

nor vs. *or*

Nor is a conjunction always used in the negative, usually before the second or last of a set of negative possibilities, after 'neither'.

Alternatively, is a conjunction used to connect different possibilities. It is also specifically used when a construction has "either".

Examples:

Nor	He drinks neither wine nor beer.
Or	(i)	It is today or tomorrow.
	(ii)	He will either eat or sleep.

so vs. such

So is used with adjectives.

Such with structures involving nouns.

Examples:

| So | Henning is so lovely. |
| Such | Arndt is such a lovely guy. |

see vs. Watch

See means to be aware of what is around you by using your eyes.

Watch means to look at something for a period of time, especially something that is changing or moving.

Examples:

| See | I can see the smoke from here. |
| Watch | I watched the football. |

stationary vs. Stationery

Stationary means standing still or not moving see

Stationery means the items needed for writing, such as paper, pens, pencils, and envelopes.

Examples:

| Stationary | The vehicle was stationary. |
| Stationery | We need to budget for stationery as consumable in the project. |

make vs. do

Do is used for any process or continuous activity

Make is used with single products.

Examples:
Do   I do the shopping every Monday.
Make   Last night, I made the dinner alone.

me vs. My

Me is used as the object of a verb or preposition. One uses "me" to refer to oneself. It is also used in short answers.
My is a possessive adjective.
Examples:
Me   He gave me all the data from the uranium experiment.
My   My experiment did not work out as I expected.

personal vs. personnel

Personal is an adjective. It can mean relating to or belonging to someone. It can also relate to someone's private life, including relationships and feelings.
Personnel is a noun and it refers to people who work for an organisation.
Examples:
Personal   (i)Your personal belongings are the things that belong to you.
               (ii) The book is personal.
               (iii) He uses a personal computer.
Personnel   Military personnel are the members of an army

practice vs. practise

Practice is a noun
Practise is a verb
Examples:
Practice   We need to put these ideas into practice.
Practise   We practise English speaking every day.

raise vs. rise

Raise is a transitive verb that requires an object (i.e. something else is needed to raise something).
Rise is an intransitive verb that it does not take an object (i.e. Something rises by itself).
Examples:
Raise   If you have a question, raise your hand.
        The government is going to raise the taxes by 3%.

Rise   The sun rises in the east.

The chairperson always rises to the occasion.

emigrate vs. immigrate

Emigrate refers to leave one's country of origin. One who is leaving one's old country is an emigrant.

Immigrate refers to coming into another country. One, who arrives in the new country is an immigrant.

(One who emigrates also immigrates)

Examples:

Emigrate   They emigrated from Malawi to Canada.

Immigrate   They immigrated to Canada from Malawi.

altar vs. alter

Altar refers to the sacred shrine or place of worship.

Alter means to change.

Examples:

Altar   Martin and Msau exchanged vows before the altar.

Alter   We promised never to alter our love for each other.

there vs. their

There can be used as an adjective of place. It can also be used as the introductory subject in a sentence.

Their is a possessive pronoun, like "her" or "our".

Examples:

There   The car is over there in the car park.

Their   Their manuscript has some grammar mistakes.

disinterested vs. uninterested

Disinterested means impartial.

Uninterested means being unconcerned with or having no desire to know about something.

Examples:

Disinterested   This dispute should be mediated by a disinterested person.

Uninterested   He did not want to take part because he was completely uninterested in the issues involved.

say vs. tell

Say is often used in direct speech. When used in indirect (reported) speech, it is followed by "that", but without an object. It can also be used as an adjective when it comes before the name of a person or thing one has already mentioned.

Tell is normally used in reported speech. It is used to talk about what people say, as a result, it is followed by an object and "that". When told has the meaning of "instruct", it can be followed by an object and an infinitive.

Examples:

Say   "I am sorry", said the rapist.
            The criminal said that he was sorry.
            The said journal rejected the article.
Tell   I told him that I would be late.
            He told me to leave.

what vs. which

What is used to ask a question when there are an unknown number or infinite possibilities for an answer.

Which is used if one is choosing between two items, already defined, in a different sentence. Use which when you have a very small or limited field to choose from.

Examples:

What   What movie did you go to see?
Which   Which shoes should I wear with this dress - my blue ones or
            my black ones?

compose vs. comprise

Compose refers to the constituent parts of a thing – parts that constitute or form a unit thing

Comprise means to consist of; be composed of, to include; or contain.

Examples:

The Institute of General Ecology and Environmental Protection has three chairs of professorship, namely the Chair for Nature cCnservation, the Chair for General Ecology, and the Chair for Environmental and Systems Analysis.

Compose   Institute of General Ecology and Environmental
            Protection is composed of the Chair for Nature
            Conservation, Chair for General Ecology, and the Chair
            for Environmental and Systems Analysis.

Comprise	Chair for Nature Conservation, Chair for General Ecology, and the Chair for Environmental and Systems Analysis comprise the Institute of General Ecology and Environmental Protection.

which vs. That

Which is used when what follows offers no new information, in which case it is parenthetical and requires a comma;

That is used when what follows delineates the object from some population.

Examples

Which	Wrong	We determined the organic partition of arsenic in the sediment that will define the permanent immobilisation.
	Right	We determined the organic partition of arsenic in the sediment, which will define the permanent immobilisation.
That	Wrong	The compound, which was interfering with the phenol spectrum, has been identified.
	Right	The compound that was interfering with the phenol spectrum has been identified.

it's vs. Its

It's is a contraction for "it is".

Its is possessive.

Examples:

It's	It's Friday again.
Its	The baby was sucking its tool.

travel vs. trip vs. voyage vs. journey

Travel can be used in general terms as a verb to means changing location. The word travel is very rarely used as a noun.

Trip is a noun often used when the travelling distance is short. Mostly, it is used in connection with business.

Trip is a verb in the context of travelling because, as a verb, it has a very different meaning. It means to nearly fall over.

Voyage is usually a long journey by boat. The word voyage is very rarely used as a verb.

Journey is the 'piece' of travel between two or more points. The word journey is very rarely used as a verb.

Examples:

Travel	I have to travel a lot for work.
Trip	How was your trip?
	I have to travel a lot for work. I am off on another business trip next week.
Voyage	The voyage to South Africa took over six weeks.
Journey	The journey from Dresden to Tharandt takes 19 minutes by train.

when vs. If

If states a condition. Use of if indicates that one does not know whether or not an action will happen.

When indicates a time. This means one is sure an activity will be finished, but only after another activity had taken place.

Example:

When	When I am finished with my work, I will help you.
If	If you find some mistakes, please let me know.

cloth vs. clothe vs. clothes

Cloth is the material for making clothes.

Clothes is what one wears.

Clothe is a verb of action when one puts on clothes.

Examples:

Clothes	Chizi does not like his best clothes.
Cloth	Chizi brings pieces of cloth everyday from school.
Clothe	Chimango is always well clothed

bath vs. bathe

Bath is a noun, what one takes.

Bathe is a verb, the action one does when taking or giving a bath.

Examples:

Bath	Nitesh is taking a bath once a day.
Bathe	Luvuyo bathes every night.

very vs. Too

Very, placed before an adjective and adverb, means more than enough.

Too placed before an adjective and adverb, means more than enough; to a higher degree than is necessary. It can only be used with a positive adjective if the context makes it clear that there is something negative in the situation, as in the example below.

Examples:

Very   He is a very tall man. He is very tall.

Too   It is too hot a day to play tennis.

                It is too strange a story to be true.

accident vs. incident

Accident is used to describe things that happen unintentionally.

Incident refers to the occurrence of a thing which can be both accidentl or intentional actions, such as crimes.

Examples:

Accident   The accident occurred when the bus was negotiating a sharp corner.

Too   22 people have been killed in an incident that occurred yesterday afternoon at a uranium mine.

admit vs. recognise vs. accept

Admit is to agree unwillingly that something is true or that someone else is right. It also means to allow someone to enter a public place or to join an organization.

Recognize is to know who someone is or what something is because you have seen, heard, experienced, or learned about them in the past. It also means to officially accept that an organization, government, document, etc. has legal or official authority, and to be thought of as being important or very good by a lot of people.

Accept means to take something that someone offers you, or agree to do something that someone asked you to do.

Examples:

Admit   He admitted to have illegally downloaded music from the Internet.

Recognize   She was humming a tune I did not recognize.

                His certificate was recognized in his home country.

                He is recognized as a genius.

Accept   Chimango accepted the birthday invitation.

and vs. Or

And is used when two or more thing add up to one sense or issue.

Or is used to indicate choices when one among many things is the sense or the issue.

Examples:

| And | He has a car and a bicycle. |
| Or | I do not know whether he has a car or a bicycle. |

learn vs. Study

Study describes an activity, the activity that you undertake when you want to learn about something.

Learn focuses on the moment when something has become part of one's knowledge. It also contains a sense of completion and permanency; usually when one has learned something, you know everything about it and one does not easily forget it.

Examples:

| Learn | I learned how to play the piano. |
| Study | I studied German for three years, but I can't speak it. |

realize vs. notice

Realise means to know and understand the importance of something. It is a cognitive event, something that involves thinking about a situation. Notice means to see, hear, or feel something. It is more of a physical event in which something comes to our attention through our senses. It is possible to notice something without realizing that it is important.

Examples:

Realise	Do you realize that you are an hour late?
	I realize how much she means to you.
Notice	He spilled the coffee, but Karin did not notice.
	Abukari may notice a numb feeling in his fingers.
	He was too tired to even notice how tired and hungry he was.

continuous vs. continual

Continuous means unbroken, so that something that occurs continuously occurs with no breaks.

Continual describes something that occurs repeatedly over a period.

Examples

| Continuous | We heard a continuous ringing of the fire alarm. |
| Continual | The continual ringing of the alarm indicates there is an accident. |

there vs. their vs. they're

    There indicates a place. It is the opposite of "here".

    Their is the possessive of "they".

    They're is a contraction of "they are".

    Examples:

Their	The mobility of metals depends on their chemical properties.
There	The radiation hot spot is not there.
	There are two radiation hotspots.
They're	They're are going to determine uranium concentration using ICP-MS.

sensuous vs. sensual

    Sensual refers to a preoccupation with gratifying the senses or appetite.

    Sensuous refers merely to those objects that can be perceived by the senses.

    Examples:

Sensual	His seminars are sensual.
Sensuous	The power point presentation had a sensuous quality.

lose vs. Loose

    Loose is a noun and it is pronounced loose

    Lose is a verb and it is pronounced looze

    Examples:

Lose	If the acid gets into the eyes, one can lose the eye.
Loose	The belt of my lab coat is loose.

chose vs. choose

    Chose is the past tense of the irregular verb choose

    Examples:

Chose	He chose to major in chemistry.
Choose	I choose the best quality of shoes for my children.

discrete vs. discreet

    Discrete means separate and distinct.

    Discreet means tactful, prudent, or circumspect.

    Examples:

Discrete	These are discrete projects, and their funding records should be kept separate.
Discreet	One cannot be discreet with the radiation toxicity.

dissociate vs. disassociate

Dissociate is the older word, whereas disassociate is a newcomer that has a less distinguished pedigree.

Disassociate is preferred when it talks about people.

Dissociate is preferred mostly sciences.

Examples:

Dissociate	Once salt is put in water, it dissociates into cation and anion.
	The dissociation factor of a salt can help deliver the solubility index.
Disassociate	He disassociated himself from the rumours.

incredible vs. incredulous

Incredible means unbelievable.

Incredulous means disbelieving.

Anything unbelievable could be called incredible;

but only a disbelieving person can be described as incredulous.

Examples:

Incredible	The article about human cloning was incredible.
Incredulous	I was naturally incredulous to the news that our article was off the scope of the journal.

eminent vs. imminent

Eminent means outstanding, distinguished, or noteworthy.

Imminent means impending, about to happen.

Examples:

Eminent	Prof. Pedius is eminent in the field of nanotechnology.
Imminent	Unfortunately, his retirement is imminent.

site vs. Cite

Site means place or location.

Cite means to mention.

Examples:

site	The **site** for construction of High Court has been found.
cite	Remember to **cite** the source of information in the article always.

refereed vs. referred

Refereed is an adjective qualifying an object that was referred – given to third person for evaluation and opinion on the object.

Referred is the past tense of verb "refer".

Examples:

Refereed	It is worth to publish in refereed journals.
Referred	The journal editor referred the article to the reviewer.

later vs. Latter

Later means coming, or occurring after something or time.

Latter mean coming, or occurring after another thing or person.

Examples:

Later	He came later than John did.
Latter	Both John and Mary came. The former was cycling while the latter was driving.
	In the latter days, our son was always ill.

5.4. OTHER MATTERS OF STYLE PREFERENCE BUT NOT MISTAKES

although vs. though

Both are supporting conjunctions, technically interchangeable. Although begins a clause, both at the beginning and in the middle of a sentence.

Though is used as a synonym for "however".

Examples:

Not preferred	Though no example has been found, ...
Preferred	Although no example has been found, ...
	No example has been found, though.

alternate vs. alternative

These both stem from the Latin word alter, meaning "other". However, because "alternate" can also be a verb and generally connotes vacillation, "alternative" is preferred.

Examples:

Not preferred	(i)	An alternate proof is as follows.
	(ii)	Alternately, we can prove this as follows. been found, ...
Preferred	(i)	An alternative proof is as follows.

(ii)	Alternatively, we can prove this as follows.

5.5. CHAPTER COMPENDIUM

This chapter looked at common flows, which I found and recorded while proofreading, editing, and peer-reviewing manuscripts. However, I added some more examples from everyday life that I cam across while talking to people, reading newspapers, as well as surfing for information on the Internet. Therefore, the flaws listed here can be arbitrarily categorized into three groups *vis* errors committed in writing by most scientists regardless of English being the first or second language, the general errors by ESL scientists, and finally errors common only to German speaking scientific writes. The biggest flaw in scientific writing is plagiarism, which is committed, in most cases unknowingly. It seems the Internet age has facilitated the practice of cutting-and-pasting. As a result, both ESL and EFL scientist, and both novice and veterans cut information from the websites and paste with little editing and modification. By reading this chapter, we learn that we sometimes use words or phrases wrongly without notice. Some errors were not even clear to me until I consulted some specific dictionaries on the words and phrases.

Chapter 6

CONCLUDING ADVICE

"Publish or perish (PoP)" is reality in the modern-day academia. It is also undisputable that English has become the lingua franca for sciences. Publishing of scientific findings has become so competitive that the mere novelty of research findings is not the only criteria journal editors are pursuing to evaluate the submitted manuscripts for the consideration of publication. Language quality has increasingly become a criterion. Good English is critical in science writing. However, the challenge remains that the evaluation of language quality puts scientific writers of EFL and those of ESL on the same yardstick. Thus, ESL scientists have to strive extra hard to publish internationally and report their interesting findings to the international scientific audience.

6.1. Communication with Precision and Impact

There is more to scientific writing than high-quality research. Research findings and conclusions must be communicated precisely and concisely. Poor writing skills lead to misimpression and misinterpretation. A well-written scientific paper explains the scientist's motivation for doing an experiment, the experimental design, and execution, and the meaning of the results. Scientific papers should be written in a style that is exceedingly clear and concise. The purpose of scientific communication is to inform an audience about an important finding or advancement, and to document the particular approach used to come up with the findings.

Generally, scientists should try to be very concise, and their English should be better than that in other academic disciplines. Scientific papers are written frequently in a standard format, which allows researchers to present information clearly and concisely. However, there are short-cuts and various deviations from the standard formats, hence, what is written in this book should just lay a foundation for novice scientific writers. As the novice scientific writers become veterans, they may find the best way to write scientific papers. At that point, it is the interest of this author to receive advice to shape the book in the best way possible.

6.2. COMMUNICATING IN ANOTHER LANGUAGE

Generally, science writers need to maintain conformity to publication standards, as well as other elements. More than just correcting English grammar and syntax, science writers have the task of keeping the overall quality and readability of the documents. However, writing good scientific reports is generally easier than mastering conversation in English. Many colleagues and students, who would not even complete a perfect sentence in English, would surprisingly write scientific papers with a very good quality of English. I presume that many people are destructed by being very mindful of mistakes, and as a result, they are tense and fail to speak a completely correct sentence. While writing, they have invisible audience and have time to correct their mistakes.

In their career, scientist should present presentations in English in different scientific gatherings. Thus, mastering speaking English is equally important because it will not only help speak in the conference, but also tremendously assist in improving scientific writing skills for most ELS. Thus, in this concluding advice, I will take the reader to the peripheral of the subject of the current book, and advise how developing skills in scientific writing in English would benefit in mastering English as a Second Language. Mastering speaking English and scientific writing in English require three things, vis a vis patience, humility, and adaptability.

6.2.1. Patience

Learning a new language can take time. Similarly, ESL scientist should not expect to write perfectly after reading this book. They need patience and practice. Unlike children who can easily learn two or more languages simultaneously by just being exposed to them, adults usually find learning a new language much more difficult. It is more difficult for scientist because they usually have busy schedules, and other pursuits, such as mastering languages like English are, in most cases, put on hold.

6.2.2. Humility

Scientists of ESL whose command of English is poor must not give up speaking the language. They should be courageous and shed some of their own self-importance, ego, and worries about dignity to make progress. They should write and let competent people comment on their writing. They should never get offended at the criticisms they may encounter. If they do not make mistakes, then they are not using their English enough.

6.2.3. Adaptability

Because learning a new language often means learning a new culture, it helps to be adaptable. ESL scientist should have an open mind to learning English. It should be realised that English is not necessarily better than the others are, but just different. Thus, it is advisable to reach out to make friends with people who speak fluent English because language skills are acquired the way chicken eat – eating grain by grain. The little specks are not much in themselves, but they keep adding up. Thus, every time one speaks to a fluent speaker or writes a scientific article in English, one learns a new way of expression and use of words or if not new vocabulary. Further, regular devotion of short of time to study is more effective than in frequently setting aside large chunks of time. It is worth to keep in mind that there are no shortcuts around personal effort and perseverance.

6.3. Plateaus for Novice Scientific Writers

When I started self-teaching and learning in scientific communications and writing, I felt at times that I was stuck on a plateau, struggling at the same level without seeing any improvement. This was mainly because as much as I tried to implement what I learned in to perfect scientific writing and good English, my manuscripts kept on being rejected by journals, with review comments bordering poor language quality. It was so frustrating, as I considered myself a quartz-native

English speaker, for one, and secondly, I had put extra effort into learning skills in scientific writing. I might not be the only one who found myself in such a frustrating and demotivating circumstance. Many other scientific writers do find themselves having similar feelings, where they feel the effort they give to perfect their writing skills does not have an equal return. If such a feeling arises, what should be done?

First, as scientists, we should reflect on the reasons for learning to write scientific papers in a second language, English. Reflecting on the prime goals or purpose reinforces the resolve.

Second, we should have reasonable expectations. As an ESL writer, one should never compare with an EFL in writing and even when speaking. This is the point of being a scientific writer; one wants the audience to be able to understand in the simplest way. Therefore, ESL contributors should focus on communicating clearly using what they have already learned.

Third, look for milestones to gauge their own progress. It may be disappointing because improvements in scientific writing, likewise in English, is like watching grass grow – one does not notice the growth, but day by day, the grass gets higher. Nevertheless, advancement is always seen when one looks at where they started. The most important thing to do is to avoid judging one's progress by that of others.

Fourth, view the process as a long-term investment. The best would be to look at how a three- or four-year-old child communicates. -Three year-olds do not use sophisticated words and complex grammar, yet, they can carry on a basic conversation. Analogically, novice scientific writers should not strive on writing complicated or flowerily statements. They should use simple vocabulary and grammar to write their articles. It is easier to connect simpler sentences than to simplify long, complicated sentences.

Fifth, use English as much as possible. Naturally, it can be frustrating to try to communicate when one has a limited vocabulary. I found it very frustrating when I was learning German, however, the very frustration can motivate one to persevere. For instance, when I was learning German, I hated being at a level where I could not understand presentations, stories, and jokes. The feelings pushed me to work harder to pass through the stage and learn German.

6.4. Use Good Colleague-ness of Veteran Scientific Writers

What can those who are EFL and have good scientific writing skills do to help novice English scientific writers? Likewise, how should journal editors and reviewers advise contributors of ESL constructively? In my view, the conduct of professional and EFL scientific writers, reviewers, and editors play a very important role in shaping novice scientific writers. Professional writers, or EFL, should try as much as possible to write concisely or speak slowly but correctly when interacting with novice or ESL writers. They should never imitate mistakes or try to reduce their writing standard and quality to the same level as the ESL or novice writers. When speaking, fluent EFL should avoid finishing sentences for ESL learners. Further, bilingual professionals, when given a manuscript to proofread, should never give any comments in any language other than English, despite the fact that they may speak the same language as the author. Like any other learners, novice scientific writers cherish genuine critiques for their efforts. Therefore, proofreaders, editors, and reviewers should, in most cases, avoid discouraging comments and asking questions in the manuscripts. For instance, a reviewer wrote, "what the hell is the language here" and "this is nonsense and it is not English". A good proofreader, reviewer, or editor should suggest the best way to write or express such a statement.

6.5. Write with Peer-reviewer's Expectation

As already mentioned at the beginning of this book, I have served as a peer reviewer for a number of journals. Hence, this book should end by sharing with the readers the philosophy which makes me accept close to a hundred reviews invitations in a year, and what I, as a reviewer, usually look for in a manuscript. As a scientific writer, we should know what reviewers usually think and expect from our manuscript so that we can write knowing exactly what to include and what to avoid.

6.5.1. Philosophy of Peer Reviewing of Manuscripts

My philosophy as a reviewer is that my job as a reviewer is not like others. Publishing research findings and the reviewing process are supposed to benefit the author as much as the editor to maintain a certain standard of scientific discussion. I believe that authors deserve detailed feedback in a non-hostile tone, regardless of whether I recommend rejecting, revising, or accepting their work. By agreeing to review, I take on the responsibility of doing a thorough job. Thus, I try, as much as possible, to review objectively and with high quality, just the way I would wish others to review my manuscripts. If I feel that I cannot commit to my review philosophy, I turn the invitation down because it is unforgivable to do a poor job, and establish a bad reputation.

I believe that the authors are the masters of their work and the research that proceeds it. On the other hand, readers have the right to read good and well thought through pieces. Therefore, authors have the responsibility of submitting mature manuscripts. Submission of premature manuscripts, and manuscripts that are not well thought through, puts me off easily. I wish authors would realize that I volunteer time from a busy schedules to conduct thorough reviews, and I am always thrilled to do so for well thought through pieces. I also lean from such manuscripts.

6.5.2. Peer Reviewing Process

Usually, I go through a manuscript three times. The first is to learn the subject mater; the second is to read the manuscript in depth to analyze and digest each sentence, and finally to actually edit it and write the specific critiques. When reporting my criticisms, I always split my review critiques into two sections:

(i) General comments on the manuscript in which I analyze and comment on the overall worthiness, readability, and style of presentation of the manuscript; and

(ii) Specific comments on individual passages in the manuscript. Under specific comments, the comments are very detailed so that the authors benefit from them as much as possible. I usually provide comments clearly referencing the page, section, and paragraph or line number.

Reviewers' critiques are merely intended to help authors revise and publish quality work. From reviewing, I have noted little reason for poor manuscript writing, which include:

a) Authors failing to explain themselves clearly. Consequently, the concepts, motivation, background, actual results, and contributions do not come across well. In such circumstance, my job as a reviewer is to look for the technical innovation in the manuscript. Depending on the innovation and novelty of the technical content of the manuscript, I recommend for massive revision or rewriting the paper;

b) Sometimes, the research may be of low quality or not a significant contribution. The research may be too premature to publish and was submitted hastily in order to meet deadlines, or may not fit the characteristics of the intended journal. Such manuscripts have massive spelling, typographic syntax, and even grammatical errors. The manuscript requires drastic proofreading. My recommendation to the editor depends on whether the errors are committed because of carelessness and laziness, or accidentally.

6.5.3. Expectations of a Peer Reviewer

When reviewing, there a set of guidelines that peer reviewers follow in order to evaluate the manuscript objectively. Usually, respective journals provide basic guidelines tailored to meet the quality and scope of the journal. The rest are based on the reviewer's knowledge of the subject and principle of scientific writing, including English. Thus, it is important for authors to know the main issues reviewers look for in a manuscript. Below are questions most reviewers ask when reviewing a manuscript. Not all of the guidelines may apply universally for all manuscripts.

#	Questions
1	Does the title address and cover what the manuscript really discusses?
2	Can a reader get the overview of the study by reading the abstract? What was the motivation and question answered by the study? How was the study conducted, what was found, and what was learned from the study?
3	Does the manuscript cover everything promised in the introduction? Is the motivation of the study adequately provided?
4	Are all descriptions clear? Are the tables and figures clear? Do they make sense on their own or only if one has read the text carefully? Are there too many descriptions? Would an additional table or figure help? Would an example help?
5	Are the research contributions clear? Are the contributions significant?
6	Is the approach clearly explained and well laid out? Does the author

	justify each of the points made?
7	Are the equations, algorithms, methods, experiments, and conclusions correct, robust, comprehensive, and sensible?
8	Is the research properly grounded in the literature?
9	Has the author expressed the limitations of the research and the author's approach?
10	Has the author performed a complete analysis and drawn insightful conclusions?
11	Has the author described his or her future research plans? Is it clear where the research described in this paper will lead and what the next step will be?
12	Is the conclusion significant? Is it just a rehash of the paper? Does it provide new synthesis or insights? Does it leave the reader excited about the research, the research domain or the future?
13	Do the authors use important, current, and adequate citations? Are there too many citations? Are any irrelevant or insignificant? Are they at an adequate level for the publication (e.g., research oriented vs. trade journals; technical reports vs. journal articles)? Are there too many citations to the author's own work? Can you suggest any missing citations the author may have overlooked?
14	How is the author's writing style? Is it too "dense" to make sense? Does it keep the reader's interest? Is it too informal? Note that an informal style in itself sometimes is very effective in getting a paper's ideas across. Similarly, many authors use humour very effectively in research papers. Only if the informality or humour gets in the way, should it be discouraged. (On the other hand, there are certain fields, which enforce very formal writing styles, in which an informal style is deemed inappropriate.)

6.6. RESPONSIBILITY OF THE AUTHORS

This book ends with reminding authors that they are responsible for ensuring the quality of the manuscripts regardless of being ESL or EFL. A manuscript should be submitted when thoroughly proofread. Proofreading includes checking for correct grammar, correct spelling, and overall, that a paper is readable.

German and other ESL authors can use editing institution or EFL colleagues to help in the editing process. Do not give up writing to communicate the interesting research findings, even if using English as Second Language.

Good writing is rewriting, and one should make a serious effort at editing, rewriting, and fine-tuning before you give the manuscript to anyone else to read [3, 8, 22, 32]. After completing writing, authors should put a piece of writing away for a few days before they can approach it dispassionately enough to rework it. Get colleagues or other people to read the manuscript. If they cannot understand it or understand with difficulties, then the manuscript needs to be re-worked. Publication quality of scientific writing is usually a product of the research community rather than the sole effort of the author(s): reviewers and editors make a big difference to the vast majority of published papers [1, 33, 39, 42]. Scientific writers should be accustomed both to reviewing other scientist's work and to having their own reviewed. Hence, novice authors should consider forming a mutual editing team with other scientists to review each other's work.

It is difficult to read for continuity on the computer screen because one can see so little text at any given moment [1]. It is also more difficult to flip over several pages to scan for repetition, and parallel structure. To do a good job of proofing a paper, it is advisable to read a hard copy at some point during the writing or rewriting process.

6.7. CLOSING ADVICE

This book is not a solution to all problems in English for environmental sciences for novice writers of English as a Second Language, likewise, problems in scientific communication and writing. Actually, it should be used as a starting point. There are many other sources of information in general, of which a selection has been appended in this book. Furthermore, this book provides the most generalized approach, and for specific advice, consults respective journals for guidelines. It is neither a guide nor a writing manual (if time allows, a manual will follow later). Guidelines provided by journals have the right, and all others follow.

APPENDIX

APPENDIX 1: SOME MAJOR DIFFERENCES BETWEEN THE BRITISH AND AMERICAN ENGLISH VARIETIES

Most of examples have been adapted from http://www.scit.wlv.ac.uk/~jphb/american.html with kind permission from the website owner, Mr Peter Burden. More examples and an elaborate explanation on the differences between the two varieties of English can be accessed on the website.

A1.1. Differences in Spellings

American English	British English	Remarks
aluminium	aluminium	
analog	analogue	
anesthesia	anaesthesia	
archaeology	archaeology	
bylaw	bye law	
catalog	catalogue	
centre	centre	
color	colour	
curb	kerb	Edge of roadway or pavement. "curb" in the sense of "restrain" is used in British and American English.
defense	defence	

dialog	dialogue	
donut	doughnut	"donut" is informal and is quite commonly used in British English to suggest that the bun is of a typical American character.
draft	draught	
encyclopedia	encyclopaedia	
favorite	favourite	
gage	gauge	American usage is olete
gray	grey	
gynecology	gynaecology	
hauler	haulier	
honor	honour	
humor	humour	
jewelry	jewellery	
license	licence	British usage is license for the verb and licence for the noun
maneuver	manoeuvre	
meter	metre	British usage is "meter" for a measuring device and "metre" for the unit of length.
mold	mould	
mustache	moustache	
nite	night	"nite" is informal in both American and British English
omelet	omelette	
pajamas	pyjamas	
practice	practise	British usage is "practise" for the verb and "practice" for the noun
program	programme	British usage is ."program" for computers and "programme" for television or radio.
routing	routeing	
specialty	speciality	
story	storey	of building
sulfur	sulphur	
thru	through	American usage is obsolescent but may still be seen on road signs
tire	tyre	part of wheel in contact with road
vise	vice	

A1.2. Some Grammar Differences Are Consistent between American and British

	American English	British English
	came over	came round
	different than,	different from,
	different from	different to
	Elbe River,	River Elbe,
	Shire River	River Shire
	He seems to be an intelligent man.	He seems an intelligent man.
	I [already] ate.	I have [already] eaten.
In response to: do you have?	I do	I have
	I do not	I have not
	I went	I have gone
	Lets go see a movie.	Lets go and see a movie.
	Look out the window.	Look out of the window.
	Meet with her	Meet her
	Talk with	talk to
	The house needs painting.	The house wants painting.
	to be in a sale	to be on sale
	to be on a team	to be in a team
	to live on a street	to live in a street

A1.3. Selected Vocabulary Differences between British and American English

American English	British English	American English	British English
antenna	aerial	intersection	cross roads
auto, automobile	car	kerosene	paraffin
automated teller machine (ATM)	cash point	incorporated (firms)	limited (firms)
apartment	Flat	industrial park	industrial estate
appetizer	starter hors d'oeuvre	kindergarten	nursery

area code	dialling code	last name	surname
attorney	lawyer	lawyer, advocate, attorney	lawyer, solicitor, barrister
asphalt	Tarmac	lead (Permanent electrical wiring)	Cable
Band-Aid	sticking plaster	line	queue
bankroll	foot the bill	liquor	spirits
bar	pub, public house	lobby (Room one encounters first in a building)	foyer
beltway, loop	ring road, circular road	locker room	changing room
bill	note	lost and found	lost property
binder clip	bulldog clip	lot	plot
blinders	blinkers	love seat	settee
blinkers (turn signals)	indicators	low fat milk	semi skimmed milk
braid (hair style)	plait	lumber	timber
broad jump	long jump	mail	post
brown bag lunch	packed lunch	mail man	postman
bun (A small round loaf)	bap, roll	mail slot	letter box
bureau	chest of drawers	mall	shopping centre
busy signal	engaged tone	mass transit	public transport
cafeteria	canteen	movies	films
caravan	convoy	movie theater	cinema
cart	trolley	napkin	serviette
casket	coffin	oatmeal	porridge
cell phone, cellular phone	mobile phone	operating room	operating theatre
check	cheque	overpass (road system)	flyover
checking account	current account	pantihose/pantyhose	tights
chief executive officer (CEO)	managing director (MD)	pants	trousers
chips	crisps	paraffin	wax
comfort station	public convenience, toilet	parking lot	car park

condominium, condo	block of flats	pass	Overtake
conductor	guard	A faster vehicle *passes* a slower one	
		A faster vehicle *overtakes* a slower one	
corn	sweet corn, maize, corn-on-the-cob		
corn starch	corn flour	pastor	minister, vicar, rector
cotton batting	cotton wool	penitentiary	prison
coworker	workmate	period	full stop
		(Punctuation at end of sentence)	
crackers	biscuits	personalty	personal property
crosswalk	pedestrian crossing	powdered sugar	icing sugar
daylight saving(s) time	summer time	pre-natal	ante-natal
dead end	cul-de-sac	preserves	jam, marmalade
deep freeze	freezer	radio	wireless
delivery truck	van	railroad	railway
denatured alcohol	methylated spirits, meths	recess	break
desk clerk	receptionist	reforestation	reafforestation
dessert	pudding	rent	hire
detour	diversion	scale	weighbridge
diaper	nappy	schedule	timetable
discount	concession	scheme	plot
district attorney	public prosecutor	Scotch Tape	Sellotape
		sedan	saloon (car type)
driver's license	driving licence	semi-trailer	articulated lorry
eggplant	aubergine	server	waiter or waitress
electrician's tape	insulating tape	senior	pensioner
elementary school	primary school	shade	blind
elevator	lift	shrimp	prawn
exit (on the road)	junction	sidewalk	pavement or footpath
expressway	main road	sneakers	trainers
eyeglasses	spectacles,	soccer	football

	specs		
fair (commerce)	show	soda	soft drink
fall	autumn	sports utility vehicle (SUV)	pick up
fender	wing (car, vehicle)	store	shop
	mudguard (bicycle)	streetcar	tram
field	pitch	stub	counterfoil
firehouse	fire station	subway	underground railway
fire starter	fire lighter	suspenders	braces
fire truck	fire engine or fire appliance	teller	cashier
first floor	ground floor	thread	cotton (for sawing)
flashlight	torch	trail	track, footpath
freeway	motorway	train station	railway station
french fries	chips	two weeks	fortnight
garbage, trash	rubbish, refuse	under	cellar
		basement	
garbage can	dustbin	union suit	long johns, ombinations
garbage collector	dustman	vacation	holiday
gas	petrol	vest	waistcoat
gear shift, gear stick	gear lever	wallet	purse
generator	dynamo	water heater	immersion heater, geyser
goaltender	goalkeeper	welfare	benefit
grade	gradient (slope)	well-to-do	well-off
grade crossing	level crossing	White-out (correcting fluid)	Tippex
ground (electrical)	earth (electrical)	wrench	spanner
ground (e.g. meat)	minced (e.g. meat)	yard	garden
headlamp	headlight (car)	zip code	post code
high school	secondary school	zipper	zip
instalment plan	hire purchase	zucchini	courgette

APPENDIX 2. WAYS TO PRESENT RESULTS

Example 1

An examination of the concentration of uranium in the medium and the amount of exudation from *Lemna Gibba* revealed a positive or direct correlation between increasing uranium concentration and the amount of DOC exuded. An analysis using Pearson's correlation coefficient supported this observation, $r(120) = 0.85$, $p < 0.001$.

Example 2

The control culture experiment accumulated more arsenic (mean = 167.1 $\pm$ 45.3 mg kg^{-1}) during the bioaccumulation test than the PO_4^{3-} culture (M = 92.3 $\pm$ 25.3 mg kg^{-1}). This difference was tested using an independent groups t test, and was shown to be significant, $t(12) = 1.23$, $p = 0.283$. Thus, the data support the notion of a phosphate effect on arsenic bioaccumulation by *Lemna gibba*.

Example 3

The mean scores for the short, medium, and long retention intervals were 5.9, 10.3, and 14.2, respectively. A one way analysis of variance revealed a significant effect of retention interval, $F(2, 34) = 123.07$, $p < 0.001$.

Example 4

While the biosorption of uranium by oven-dried *Lemna gibba* biomass was 60%, only 35% did in live biomass. A 2 x 2 Chi Square analysis revealed that this was a significant difference, $x2$ $(1, N = 119) = 10.51$, $p = 0.0012$, suggesting that there was a relationship between biomass pre-treatment and biosorption capacity.

APPENDIX 3. EXAMPLES OF FIGURE AND TABLE PRESENTATION

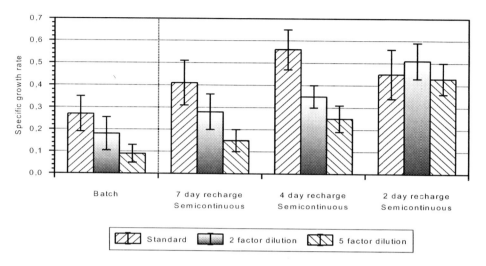

Figure 1. Mean maximum specific growth rates of *Lemna gibba* in Hutner Nutrient media of different dilution factors after 21-day growth. Values are mean of 4 replicates and error bars are standard deviation.

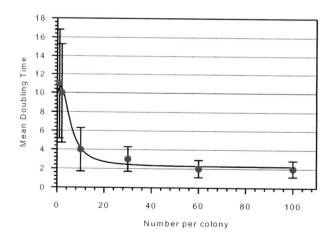

Figure 2. Mean of doubling time for different colony sizes of *Lemna gibba* in standard Hutner solution in a 21-day culture period. The results are mean of four replications, and the error bars are standard deviations.

Table 1. Mean Content of Selected Cations and Anions of Importance in Tailing Waters of Two Abandoned Uranium Mines and Their Corresponding Literature Values for Natural Surface Waters

	Concentrations (mg l^{-1})			
	Lengenfeld	Mechelgrün	Literature	
			Values	Source
P	<0.1	0.01± 0.003	~0.02	Wetzel (2001)
Ca	54.0±	87.0 ± 12.6	1.0 – 2.0	Wetzel (2001)
K	10.0±	12.6 ± 3.4	2.0 – 3.0	Wetzel (2001)
Mg	12.6±	42.8 ± 9.4	~4.0	Wetzel (2001)
NH_4^+	1.6 - 3.5	1.1 ± 0.6	~0.1 – 0.5	Wetzel (2001)
NO_3	10.0 - 30.0	60.6 ± 13.2	3.0 – 4.7	Wetzel (2001)
Fe	<0.2	<0.1	0.5 – 1.0	Wetzel (2001)
BO_3	-	0.34 ± 0.08	~0.01	Wetzel (2001)
SO_4^{2-}	140.0 - 420.0	105.0 ± 20.05	>300.0	Kalff (2002)
Cu	-	0.005 ± 0.001	~0.007	Wetzel (2001)
Mn	-	4.4 ± 1.2	~0.007	Wetzel (2001)
Zn	-	~0.02	~0.02	Wetzel (2001)
Cl^-	20.7 ± 7.6	55.0 ± 11,9	>120.0	Kalff (2002)
Co	-	0.002 ±0.0005	0.002	Streit (1992)
Mo	-	0.01 ±0.005	~0.001	Streit (1992)

Values presented for Lengenfeld were sampled from September to November 2001, and for Mechelgrün were sampled from February to June 2002.

APPENDIX 4. RECOMMENDED FURTHER READING

Books and Guides on Scientific Writing

Paradis J.G. and Zimmerman M.L. (1997) *The MIT Guide to Science and Engineering Communication.* Cambridge, Mass.: MIT Press.

Provost G. (1995) *100 Ways to Improve Your Writing: Proven Professional Techniques for Writing Style and Power,* Mentor Books, Dublin.

Bates R.L., Adkins-Heljeson M.D. Buchanan R.C. eds., (1995) *Geowriting: A guide to writing, editing, and printing in the Earth Sciences,* 5th ed.: Alexandria, VA, American Geological Institute, 80 p.

Beall H. and Trimbur J. (2000) *A Short Guide to Writing about Chemistry* (2nd Edition) Longman, London, New York, Hong Kong.

Chambers H. (2001) *Effective Communication Skills: For Scientific and Technical Professionals,* Perseus Books Group, New York.

Cribb J. and Hartomo S. (2002) *Sharing Knowledge: a Guide to Effective Scientific Communication,* Csiro Publishing, Collingwood, Victoria.

Day R.A. (1998) *How to Write and Publish a Scientific Paper:* 5th Edition, Oryx Press Westport.

Dodd J.S. (1997) *The ACS Style Guide: A Manual for Authors and Editors,* 2 edition, (An American Chemical Society Publication; New York.

Garson G.D. (2002) *Guide to writing empirical papers, theses, and dissertations:* New York, Marcel Dekker, Inc., 350 p.

Hacker D. (2000). A pocket style manual, 3rd ed.: Boston, MA, Bedord Books, 233 p. Hacker, D., 2000, *Rules for writers,* 4th ed.: Boston, MA, Bedford Books, 499 p.

Matthews J.R., Bowen J.M. and Matthews R.W. (2000). *Successful Scientific Writing: A Step-by-Step Guide for the Biological and Medical Sciences,* Cambridge University Press, Cambridge.

Montgomery S.L. (2002). *The Chicago Guide to Communicating Science: Chicago,* University of Chicago Press, 228 p.

Pechenik J. (1997). *A short guide to writing about biology* (3rd ed.). New York: Addison-Wesley.

Rathbone R.R. (1985). *Communicating Technical Information: A New Guide to Current Uses and Abuses in Scientific and Engineering Writing* 2nd edition Addison-Wesley, München.

Schoenfeld R. (2001) *The Chemist's English: Say It in English, Please!* 3rd rev. ed. Viley-VCH Verlag GmbH Weinheim.

Seely J. (2004) *Oxford A - Z of Grammar and Punctuation,* Oxford University Press, Oxford, London, New York.

Strunk Jr. W. and White E.B. (1979). *The elements of style* (3rd ed.). New York: MacMillan.

Strunk Jr. W. 2000, *The elements of style,* 4th ed.: Ithaca, New York , Press of W.P. Humphrey, 43 p.

Zinsser W. (1998). *On writing well* (6th ed.). New York: Harper Collins.

Rathbone R.R. (1985) *Communicating Technical Information: A New Guide to Current Uses and Abuses in Scientific and Engineering* Writing 2nd edition Addison-Wesley, München.

Schoenfeld R. (2001) *The Chemist's English: Say It in English, Please!* 3rd rev. ed. Viley-VCH Verlag GmbH Weinheim.

Strunk Jr. W. (2000) *The elements of style,* 4th ed.: Ithaca, New York, Press of W.P. Humphrey, 43 p.

Yang J.T: (1995) *An Outline of Scientific Writing: For Researchers with English as a Foreign Language.* World Scientific Publishing. London 160p.

English Language and Grammar in General

Burchfield R. W. and Fowler, H. W. (1996) *The New Fowler's Modern English Usage.* Clarendon Press.

Hewings M. (2005) A*dvanced Grammar in Use with Answers,* Cambridge University Press, Cambridge, London.

Stilman A. (2004) *Grammatically Correct: The Writer's Essential Guide to Punctuation,* Spelling, Style, Usage and Grammar, Writers Digest Books New York.

Seely J. (2004) *Oxford A - Z of Grammar and Punctuation,* Oxford University Press, Oxford, London, New York.

Shaw H. (1993) *Errors in English and Ways to Correct Them, HarperCollins Publisher,* New York, London.

Shaw H. (1996) *Punctuate It Right, HarperTorch Publisher,* New York, London.

Further Reading on Plagiarism

(a) books

Angelil-Carter S. (2000). *Stolen Language? Plagiarism in Writing.* Harlow, UK: Pearson Education.

Buranen L. and Roy A.M. eds. (1999) *Perspectives on Plagiarism and Intellectual Property in a Postmodern World.* Albany: SU of New York.

Hacker D. (2002) *A Writer's Reference. Fifth Edition.* Boston & New York: St. Martin's/Bedford,

Harmon W. (2002) *A Handbook to Literature. Ninth Edition.* Upper Saddle River, NJ: Prentice Hall.

Howard R.M. (1999) S*tanding in the shadow of giants: Plagiarists, authors, collaborators.* Stamford, CT: Ablex Publishing.

Murfin R. and Supryia M. Ray. 2003. *The Bedford Glossary of Critical and Literary Terms.* Second Edition. Boston & New York.

(b) Recent Articles in Books and Periodicals

Anderson G.L. (1999). *Cyberplagiarism: A look at the Web term paper sites. College & Research Libraries News*, 60(5), 371-373.

Holden C. (1999). Kinder, gentler plagiarism policy? *Science,* 283(5401), 483.

Macrae C.N., Bodenhausen G.V. and Calvini, G. (1999). Contexts of cryptomnesia: May the source be with you. *Social Cognition,* 17(3), 273.

Snapper J.W. (1999). On the Web, plagiarism matters more than copyright piracy. *Ethics and Information Technology,* 1(2), 127.

(c) Some Useful Internet Sites

The websites and links may change as they are not bound with this compilation. These websites were last accessed, and were proved active in December 2008.

http://www.sfedit.net/
http://www.indiana.edu/~wts/wts/plagiarism.html
http://sis.pitt.edu/~wedmin/academics/information/sisacint.html
http://webster.commnet.edu/mla/plagiarism.htm
http://www.virtualsalt.com/antiplag.htm
http://www.sa/utoronto.ca/details.php?wscid=94
http://plagiarism.org
http://plagiarism.phys.virginia.edu
http://www.academicintegrity.org
http://www.pitt.edu/~englit/plagiarism.htm
http://www.writing.eng.vt.edu/
http://aerg.canberra.edu.au/pub/aerg/edulertz.htm

REFERENCES

[1] W.H. Guilford, Teaching peer review and the process of scientific writing, *Advances in Physiology Education* 25(2001) 67–175.

[2] C. Clark, BIO 190 - Writing an abstract, California State Polytechnic University, Pomona, 2001.

[3] J.G. Bryan, On scientific writing: The need for more conviction and subjectivity, *The Leading Edge*(1993) 246-347.

[4] K.D. Mahrer, Bugged by bad writing? Help break the cycle, *The Leading Edge*(2000) 86-87.

[5] S. Steingraber, *Guidelines for Writing Scientific Papers*, Michigan State University 1985, pp. 185-191.

[6] M.A. Morrison, *Tips on Scientific Writing*, Michael A. Morrison, 2004.

[7] S. Maloy, *Guidelines for Writing a Scientific Paper*, San Diego State University, 2001.

[8] J.A. Elefteriades, Twelve Tips on Writing a Good Scientific Paper, International. *Journal of Angiology* 11(2002) 53-55.

[9] P. Stapleton, A. Youdeowei, J. Mukanyange, H.v. Houten, Scientific writing for agricultural research scientists - *a training reference manual*, West Africa Rice Development Association(WARDA) in collaboration with the Technical Centre for Agricultural and Rural Cooperation (CTA), 1995.

[10] PWC, Style Points for Scientific Writing, Psychology Writing Center, Washington, 2004, p. 4.

[11] N.R. Cozzarelli, *Responsible authorship of papers in PNAS, PNAS* 101(2004) 10495-.

[12] R. Herbert, G.T. Allison, What constitutes authorship?, *Australian Journal of Physiotherapy* 47(2001) 225.

[13] C.A. Marco, T.A. Schmidt, Who Wrote This Paper? Basics of Authorship and Ethical Issues, *Acad Emerg Med* 11(2004) 76-77.

[14] L.B. Kasunic, *Resident Authorship: A Painless Process, American College of Osteopathic Family Physicians*, 1996, pp. 1-10.

[15] A. Sheikh, Publication ethics and the research assessment exercise: reflections on the troubled question of authorship, *J Med Ethics* 26(2000) 422-426.

[16] D. Rennie, V. Yank, L. Emanuel, When authorship fails. A proposal to make contributors accountable, *JAMA* 278(1997) 579-585.

[17] K.D. Mahrer, Ten common qualities of uncommonly effective writers, *The Leading Age*(1999) 626.

[18] D.N. Tychnin, Clean up your English - Avoiding superfluos words in scientific reporting, *ESPR* 8(2001) 227 - 229.

[19] L.M. McGlade, B. Milot, J. Scales, Eliminating jargon, or medicalese, from scientific writing., *Am J Clin Nutr.* 64(1996) 256-257.

[20] P.O. Seglen, Why the impact factor of journals should not be used for evaluating research, *BMJ* 314(1997) 497-.

[21] E. Garfield, The meaning of the Impact Factor, *International Journal of Clinical and Health Psychology* 3(2003) 363-369.

[22] S.J. Cunningham, How to … write a paper, *Journal of Orthodontics* 31(2004) 47-51.

[23] S. Weidenborner, D. Caruso, *Writing Research Papers: A Guide to the Process*, Bedford/St. Martin's, Boston and New York, 2001.

[24] S.F. Carey, Combating plagiarism, *Phi Delta Kappa Fastbacks* 514(2003) 7-32.

[25] M. Roig, Plagiarism and Paraphrasing Criteria of College and University Professors, Ethics and Behavior 11(2001) 307.

[26] R. Harris, *The Plagiarism Handbook Pyrczak Publishing*, Los Angeles, 2001.

[27] M. Randall, *Pragmatic Plagiarism: Authorship, Profit, and Power*, Univeristy of Toronto, Toronto: , 2001.

[28] P. Galus, Detecting and preventing plagiarism, *Science Teacher* 69(2002) 35.

[29] L. Renard, Cut and paste 101: Plagiarism and the Net, *Educational Leadership* 57(2000) 38-42.

[30] M.L. Bink, R.L. Marsh, J.L. Hicks, J.D. Howard, The credibility of a source influences the rate of unconscious plagiarism, *Memory* 7(1999) 293-308.

[31] A. Sterngold, Confronting plagiarism. *Change,* 36 3(2004).

[32]   J.R. McLaughlin, W.D. King, T.W. Anderson, E.A. Clarke, J.P. Ashmore, Paternal radiation exposure and leukaemia in offspring: the Ontario case-control study [published errata appear in *BMJ* 1993 Nov 13;307(6914):1257 and 1993 Dec 4;307(6917):1462], *BMJ* 307(1993) 959-966.

[33]   R.A. Day, How to Write and Publish Scientific Papers, *Mem Inst Oswaldo Cruz* 93(1998) 423-424.

[34]   S. Cogdill, J. Kilborn, *Avoiding Gender Bias in Pronouns,* The Write Place-LEO: Literacy Education Online, 1995-2005.

[35]   E. Agrell, Common mistakes in English technical writing, 2002, p. http://www.s2.chalmers.se/~agrell/mistakes.pdf.

[36]   L. Bauer, *An Introduction to International Varieties of English* Edinburgh University Press Edinburgh, 2002, 160 pp.

[37]   E.W. Schneider, *Englishes Around the World: General Studies,* British Isles, North America : Studies in Honour of Manfred Gorlach: 1 (Varieties of English Around the World General Series) John Benjamins Pub Co Amsterdam, 1997, 329 pp.

[38]   P. Trudgill, J. Hannah, *International English. A Guide to the Varieties of Standard English,* Arnold Publishers London, 2002, 192 pp.

[39]   K.D. Mahrer, Golf swings, tennis serves, and technical writing — things we can upgrade, T*he Leading Edge*(1998) 629-630.

[40]   K. Mahrer, Still writing in passive voice?, *The Leading Edge*(2005) 1137.

[41]   San Francisco Edit, Twelve Steps to Developing Effective Tables and Figures 2007, San Francisco Edit, San Francisco, 2007, p. www.sfedit.net/newsletters.

[42]   N.T. Griscom, *Your research: How to get it on paper and in print,* Pediatr Radiol 29(1999) 81-86.

[43]   K.D. Mahrer, Why manuscripts fail, according to 12 experts, *The Leading Age*(1999) 724-725.

[44]   K.D. Mahrer, Clearer sentences—Part 2, *The Leading Age*(2001) 662-663.

[45]   K.D. Mahrer, A boring test, *The Leading Age*(2000) 269-270.

[46]   K.D. Mahrer, Clearer sentences—Part 1, *The Leading Age*(2001) 547-548.

[47]   G.D. Gopen, J.A. Swan, *The Science of Scientific Writing,* American Scientist 78(1990) 550-558.

[48]   J. Wang, M.J. Kropff, B. Lammert, S. Christensen, P.K. Hansen, Using CA model to obtain insight into mechanism of plant population spread in a controllable system: annual weeds as an example, *Ecological Modelling* 166(2003) 277-286.

[49]   J. Gibaldi, MLA handbook for writers of research papers, *Modern Language Association*, New York, 1999.

[50] C. Clark, BIO 190 - *Writing an abstract,* California State Polytechnic University, Pomona, , 2001.

[51] San Francisco Edit, *Responding to Reviewers 2007,* San Francisco Edit, San Francisco, 2007, p. www.sfedit.net/newsletters.

[52] W.H. DuBay, *The Principles of Readability, Impact Information* (William H. DuBay), Costa Mesa, 2004.

[53] A.J. Meadows, The readability of physics papers, *Czechoslovak Journal of Physics* 36(1986) 89-91.

[54] K. Sander, Writing Scientific Papers in English. Von M. O'Connor and F. P. Woodford. Elsevier, Amsterdam 1975. Ca. DM 21, *Biologie in unserer Zeit* 9(1979) 159.

[55] R.A. Day, *How to write and publish a scientific paper.,* Cambridge University Press, Cambridge 1998.

[56] D.N. Tychinin, M. Mkandawire, English for Ecoscience: A Miniguide for Ex-Soviet and Eastern European Contributors, *Environmental Science and Pollution Research* 11(2004) 67.

[57] S. Dolainski, Grammar Traps: *A Handbook of the 20 Most Common Grammar Mistakes and How to Avoid Them,* Paragraph Publishers Norwich, Norfolk, 2004, 125 pp.

[58] S. Dolainski, Grammar Traps: *A Handbook of the 20 Most Common Grammar Mistakes and How to Avoid Them* Paragraph Publishers, Toluca Lake, 2004, 124 pp.

[59] F. Peck, *Misplaced and Dangling Modifiers, in: HyperGrammar,* (Ed), The Writing Centre, University of Ottawa, 2007, p. http://www.arts.uottawa.ca/writcent/hypergrammar/msplmod.html.

[60] E.A. Dornan, C.W. Dawe, *The Brief English Handbook* Harpercollins College Div, Toronto, 1996, 520 pp.

[61] E.D. Rockwell, *Suggestions for the composition of technical reports in the natural-resource sciences,* Technical Report Series, U.S. Department of Interior, National Bioloical Survey, Washiungton DC, 1994, p. 35.

[62] M.K. McCaskill, *Grammar, Punctuation, and Capitalization: A Handbook for Technical Writers and Editors,* NASA, Hampton, Virginia, 1998, 108 pp.

[63] P. Brian, *Common Errors in English,* William, James Co., Wilsonville, 1997, 256 pp.

[64] W.W. Brandt, Practice in critical reading as a method to improve scientific writing, *Science Education* 55(1971) 451-455.

INDEX

F

N

O

Q

R

T

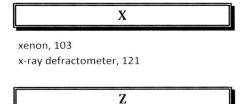

Z